French Arms Exports
The Business of Sovereignty

Lucie Béraud-Sudreau

French Arms Exports
The Business of Sovereignty

Lucie Béraud-Sudreau

IISS The International Institute for Strategic Studies

The International Institute for Strategic Studies

Arundel House | 6 Temple Place | London | WC2R 2PG | UK

First published March 2020 by **Routledge**
4 Park Square, Milton Park, Abingdon, Oxon, OX14 4RN

for **The International Institute for Strategic Studies**
Arundel House, 6 Temple Place, London, WC2R 2PG, UK
www.iiss.org

Simultaneously published in the USA and Canada by **Routledge**
52 Vanderbilt Avenue, New York, NY 10017

Routledge is an imprint of Taylor & Francis, an Informa Business

DIRECTOR-GENERAL AND CHIEF EXECUTIVE Dr John Chipman
EDITORS Dr Nicholas Redman and Dr Benjamin Rhode
ASSISTANT EDITOR Michael Marsden
EDITORIAL Vivien Antwi, Bao-Chau Pham, Sara Hussain, Jill Lally
COVER/PRODUCTION John Buck, Carolina Vargas, Kelly Verity
COVER IMAGES: Getty

The International Institute for Strategic Studies is an independent centre for research, information and debate on the problems of conflict, however caused, that have, or potentially have, an important military content. The Council and Staff of the Institute are international and its membership is drawn from almost 100 countries. The Institute is independent and it alone decides what activities to conduct. It owes no allegiance to any government, any group of governments or any political or other organisation. The IISS stresses rigorous research with a forward-looking policy orientation and places particular emphasis on bringing new perspectives to the strategic debate.

The Institute's publications are designed to meet the needs of a wider audience than its own membership and are available on subscription, by mail order and in good bookshops. Further details at www.iiss.org.

British Library Cataloguing in Publication Data
A catalogue record for this book is available from the British Library

Library of Congress Cataloging in Publication Data

ADELPHI series
ISSN 1944-5571

ADELPHI 475–476
ISBN 978-0-367-51145-6

Contents

ACKNOWLEDGEMENTS

I would like to thank Dr Nicholas Redman for his trust and support in breaking his own rule of not accepting PhD manuscripts for publication, and for helping me transform my doctoral research into an *Adelphi* book. Thanks also to Michael Marsden and Sara Hussain for their patient work in making my writing in English much more readable. Michael in particular was tireless in his devotion to the project, ensuring that my arguments were presented in the strongest possible light.

This is also an opportunity to express my gratitude to the Defence and Military Analysis Programme team at the International Institute for Strategic Studies for everything I learned from them and for the fantastic work environment they provided, on a professional and personal level, during my three and a half years with them as a research fellow for defence economics and procurement.

NOTE ON INTERVIEWS

This book is based partly on a series of interviews with individuals who were, or had been, part of the French arms-export system. Most of the interviews were conducted between 2013 and 2015 as part of my doctoral research. I spoke at length, for example, with numerous officials in different departments of the Ministry of Defence and Ministry of Foreign Affairs; with politicians, including a former defence minister; and with several executives in the defence industry.

Many of the interviews were strictly confidential and I have chosen not to name any of the individuals I spoke to – instead they are referred to as 'an official', 'a politician', 'a defence-industry executive', etc. Wherever an interviewee is quoted and in every other instance where information has been obtained directly from an interview, an endnote refers the reader to the list of interviews in the Appendix, which indicates the position the interviewee held at the time.

AP   *Agrément préalable* (Preliminary Agreement): until 2014, part of the export-licensing process for military equipment produced in France

AEMG   *Autorisation d'exportation de matériels de guerre* (Authorisation to Export War Materiel): until 2014, part of the export-licensing process for military equipment produced in France

APD   *Attestation de passage en douane* (customs certificate): until 2014, part of the export-licensing process for military equipment produced in France

ATT   Arms Trade Treaty: multilateral treaty that was adopted by the United Nations in 2013 and entered into force in 2014

Bercy   colloquial name for the Ministry of the Economy

cabinet   the office of a government minister, consisting of a team of civil servants led, typically, by political appointees, who are also referred to in this book as 'political staff'

CFSP   Common Foreign and Security Policy: legal framework for the European Union's activities relating to collective foreign-policy, defence and security matters

CIACI   Commission interministérielle d'appui aux contrats internationaux (Interministerial Commission for Supporting Civil and Military Exports): between 2007 and 2012, the entity tasked with coordinating the government's logistical support for arms exports

CIBDU   Commission interministérielle des biens à double-usage (Interministerial Commission for Dual-Use Goods)

CIEDES   Commission interministérielle pour les exportations de défense et de sécurité (Interministerial Commission for Defence and Security Exports): the forerunner to the CIACI

CIEEMG   Commission interministérielle pour l'étude des exportations de matériels de guerre (Interministerial Commission for the Study of Exports of War Materiel): the interministerial commission at the heart of the arms-export-control process within the French government bureaucracy. The acronym can also refer to the commission's monthly meetings or even, colloquially, to the arms-export-control process as a whole.

COARM   European Union Working Party on Conventional Arms Exports

COFACE   Compagnie française d'assurance pour le commerce extérieur: a credit-insurance company formerly responsible for managing

	export guarantees on behalf of the French state (the role was transferred to Bpifrance in 2016)
DAS	Délégation aux affaires stratégiques (Directorate for Strategic Affairs): forerunner to the DGRIS
deputy *(député)*	member of the National Assembly, France's lower house of parliament
DGA	Direction générale de l'armement (General Directorate for Armaments): a directorate within the Ministry of Defence, responsible for armaments acquisitions and implementing defence-industrial policy
DI	Direction du développement international (Directorate for International Development): a department within the DGA that plays the leading role in promoting arms exports. It was previously known as the DRI and, before that, the DAI.
DGRIS	Direction générale des relations internationales et de la stratégie (General Directorate for International Relations and Strategy): the successor to the DAS in 2015
EDA	European Defence Agency
Élysée	the office of the French president, whose residence is the Palais de l'Élysée
EMA	État-major des armées (Defence Staff)
ERTA	European Agreement on Road Transport
EC	European Commission
EU	European Union
ICT (Intra-Community Transfers) **Directive**	a 2009 directive from the European Union, aiming to simplify and harmonise licensing procedures for defence goods and technologies inside the EU (Directive 2009/43/EC)
ITAR	International Traffic in Arms Regulations: part of the United States' arms-export-control legislation
LoI	Letter of Intent: 1998 agreement to develop armaments cooperation between France, Germany, Italy, Spain, Sweden and the United Kingdom
LREM	La République En Marche: centrist political party founded in 2016 by Emmanuel Macron
Ministry of Defence	formal name used in this book for France's Ministère des armées
Ministry of the Economy	formal name used in this book for France's Ministère de l'économie et des finances; also referred to colloquially as Bercy

Ministry of Foreign Affairs	formal name used in this book for France's Ministère de l'Europe et des affaires étrangères; also referred to colloquially as the Quai d'Orsay
National Assembly (Assemblée Nationale)	the lower house of the French parliament
NGO	non-governmental organisation
Offices	colloquial term referring to the entities that acted as export brokers for French defence companies, mainly during the Cold War era
PNSED	*Plan national stratégique des exportations de défense* (National Strategic Plan for Defence Exports)
PS	Parti socialiste (Socialist Party): France's principal left-wing political party during most of the period covered by this book
Quai d'Orsay	colloquial name for the Ministry of Foreign Affairs
RPR	Rassemblement pour la République: right-wing political party that merged into the UMP in 2002
SBDU	Service des biens à double usage (Dual-Use Goods Office)
Senate (Sénat)	the upper house of the French parliament
SIPRI	Stockholm International Peace Research Institute
SGDSN	Secrétariat général de la défense et la sécurité nationale (Secretariat-General for Defence and National Security): an interministerial agency, under the authority of the prime minister, which participates in the design and implementation of French defence and security policy. It chairs the monthly meetings of the CIEEMG.
SOUTEX	Soutien aux exportations (Support for Exports): a small unit within the Defence Staff, created in 2007
UDF	Union pour la démocratie française: centre-right political party; renamed as the Mouvement Démocrate (MoDem) in 2007
UMP	Union pour un Mouvement Populaire: France's principal right-wing political party for much of the period covered by this book; renamed as Les Républicains (LR) in 2015
WA	Wassenaar Arrangement: multilateral regime in which participating states coordinate export regulations for dual-use goods and technologies

INTRODUCTION

At the 2013 Paris Air Show, attended by the world's biggest military and commercial aircraft manufacturers, President François Hollande made a joke as he helped the 88-year-old CEO of Dassault Aviation, Serge Dassault, to climb the stairs of an exhibition stand: 'It's the state that's supporting Dassault ... as usual,' he said.[1] His words were overheard by a journalist and caused something of a stir in the defence community, even compelling a Dassault Aviation executive to declare in the media that 'Dassault Aviation does not live at the state's expense'.[2] The quip had touched on a sensitive issue, namely the relationship the French state maintains with the country's defence industry – and specifically its substantial backing for arms exports.

The French state espouses the doctrine that arms sales are intrinsic to the country's strategic autonomy. The rationale is as follows: for France to be able to act independently in the defence and foreign-policy domains, which means not having to depend on other states when it wishes to use force, it requires its own weapons-manufacturing capacity. However, the French defence industry cannot survive on domestic orders alone: it also needs to export. Arms exports are therefore both an expression and a vital component of France's sovereignty. As the defence minister, Florence Parly, put it in 2018, 'arms exports are the business model of our sovereignty'.[3]

This doctrine has remained largely intact despite transformations in the global arms trade in the post-Cold War period caused, for example, by Europeanisation, the emergence of multilateral arms-trade norms and the liberalisation of the defence-industrial sector. Although there have been some subtle, below-the-radar changes in French arms-export policy, the overall policy direction has hardly ever been questioned. Furthermore, a vast administrative structure has been created for the purpose of implementing this doctrine – indeed, the defence bureaucracy is largely geared towards promoting arms exports. And this has become a mutually reinforcing relationship: the bureaucracy helps sustain the doctrine and in doing so it also preserves its own scope and influence.

But French arms-export policy comes at a price, because sustaining the arms industry also generates its own kind of dependency. Though France did not become strategically dependent on the United States, as Gaullists feared it would, the country's defence industry has become economically dependent on its foreign customers, some of which are authoritarian, repressive regimes. This is a potential liability for France's defence and foreign policies.

Also, at a time when European countries are committing themselves to joint defence efforts – in particular by renewing cooperative projects, whether through the European Union or at the bilateral and minilateral levels – clinging to its traditional arms-export policy may become a burden for France in its relations with key European partners. President Emmanuel Macron himself has prioritised deeper European defence cooperation, in particular with Germany. However, the differences of perspective between France and Germany pose a dilemma for French defence and armaments policy. Germany's current arms-export regulations are generally more restrictive – for example Berlin has placed an embargo on arms sales to Saudi Arabia because of its role in the war in Yemen – whereas the traditional French doctrine implies being potentially open for business with all customers unless they are subject to a United Nations arms embargo (and even that has not always been an impediment – for example France was one of the main suppliers of arms to South Africa during the apartheid era).[4] While cooperation with Germany appears indispensable if the goal is to create larger markets and build the foundations of a future European defence policy, mutual inflexibility on export policy may jeopardise Franco-German projects to jointly build, for example, combat aircraft or main battle tanks. The question, therefore, is whether France will choose increased European defence cooperation, which it has long advocated, or preserve its traditional approach to arms exports. The latter would entail continued reliance on distant customers rather than European partners, and if France maintains that course without re-examining its core assumptions or even being open to debate, the country's defence policy and strategic ambitions may eventually be undermined.

A chequered history

France's arms-export policy has succeeded in maintaining a domestic defence industry generally capable of supplying the French armed forces with the equipment they need (there are a few significant exceptions, such as uninhabited aerial vehicles), and the underlying assumption that arms sales are in the national interest has survived despite a litany of scandals over the years. To give just a few examples, these include:

L'affaire des vedettes de Cherbourg

In 1967, when President Charles de Gaulle declared an arms-export embargo against the combatants in the Six-Day War, the shipbuilding projects already under way in the port city of Cherbourg in Normandy included missile boats – *vedettes* – for Israel. Though initially the embargo only affected combat aircraft that France was going to deliver to Israel, after January 1969 it was extended to all arms sales. This prompted a reaction from Israel, which had already paid for the *vedettes* and was awaiting delivery. On Christmas Eve 1969, five missile boats vanished into the night from Cherbourg docks – and were next spotted a few days later in the Mediterranean, sailing under Israeli military command towards Haifa, which they reached on 31 December. The crux of the scandal was that the *vedettes* almost certainly could not have escaped from Cherbourg without secret complicity on the part of senior French officials, who it seems wanted to find a way of honouring the contract with Israel while preserving good relationships with Arab states.

L'affaire des Exocet

During the 1982 Falklands War, the British destroyer HMS *Sheffield* was sunk by a French-built *Exocet* anti-ship missile fired by one of the Argentine Air Force's French-built *Super Étendard* combat aircraft. The British government immediately pressured France not to allow any more missiles to reach Buenos Aires. France complied but, controversially, French *Exocet* technicians who had been in Argentina at the start of the war remained there, assisting with the maintenance of the missile systems previously delivered.[5] Though the episode put a little strain on the Franco-British relationship, it undoubtedly also showcased one of the French defence industry's most advanced products.

L'affaire Luchaire

Between 1983 and 1985 the French company Luchaire was granted licences to sell around 450,000 artillery shells to Portugal, Brazil, Thailand and Yugoslavia – but in fact the shells were destined for Iran, which of course was not only at war with Iraq at the time but also had very strained relations with the West.[6] Luchaire had presented false certificates to the French authorities, but it later transpired that Ministry of Defence officials had known what was going on. Indeed, a report ordered by defence minister André Giraud (1986–88) found that Luchaire's illicit operations had been deliberately covered up by the staff of his predecessor Charles Hernu (1981–85),[7] a conclusion corroborated by later investigations.[8] Furthermore, there were suspicions that commissions on the contracts with Iran had been paid to the Socialist Party to finance election campaigns.[9]

L'affaire des frégates de Taïwan

This episode, which had a heavy whiff of corruption and intrigue, began in 1991 when the French government authorised the sale to Taiwan of six *La Fayette*-class frigates, to be built and armed by Thomson-CSF (later to become Thales) and DCN (later to become Naval Group). The contract was signed after unauthorised commissions were paid to Taiwanese intermediaries, which possibly also led to kickbacks in France. A series of suspicious deaths and probable suicides seemed to be connected with the deal – from the head of the Taiwanese Navy's procurement office, whose body was found in the sea off Taiwan in 1993, to a former Thomson-CSF engineer, who fell to his death from the window of his Toulouse apartment in 2001. An international panel of arbitrators eventually ruled in 2010 that the Taiwanese government was owed compensation for the payment of the earlier bribes: Thales had to pay

€170 million (US$226m) and the French state itself had to pay €460m (US$610m) on behalf of DCN, which had been fully state-owned in the early 1990s.

The Taiwanese *affaire* actually marked a turning point for French arms-export policy. Although the sale of the frigates to Taiwan – followed, later in the 1990s, by *Mirage* 2000 combat aircraft – was a timely boost for the French defence industry during a period when its markets were contracting following the end of the Cold War, the exposure of dubious practices increased the pressure within the French government for an overhaul of the regulations governing sales of materiel. Indeed, it was clear from interviews conducted during the research for this book that bad memories of the Taiwanese episode lingered within the Ministry of Defence and Ministry of Foreign Affairs for many years afterwards, along with anxieties about the possibility of such a case being repeated.

President Jacques Chirac, after his election in 1995, decided to halt payments to intermediaries who had been involved in securing two important contracts: with Saudi Arabia for the sale of – again – *La Fayette*-class frigates (generally referred to as the Sawari II contract), and with Pakistan for the export of *Agosta*-class submarines. There might have been an element of self-interest in Chirac's decision, as there were suspicions that the contracts had included kickbacks to finance the presidential election campaign of his rival Edouard Balladur, but it none-theless had wide-ranging consequences. It sharply reduced the flow of arms from France to Saudi Arabia, as Riyadh restricted its orders to upgrades of existing systems and did not sign another major contract with a French supplier until the Hollande presidency (2012–17). As for the impact on rela-tions with Pakistan, an ongoing judicial investigation in France is looking into whether the bombing of a bus in Karachi in 2002, in which 15 people including 11 French naval engineers were killed, could have been the indirect result of the cessation of payments to intermediaries.[10] Meanwhile, Balladur, prime minister between 1993 and 1995, and François Léotard, his defence minister at the time, are currently due to appear before the Cour de Justice de la République, a special court that examines cases of possible ministerial misconduct, over their alleged involvement in corruption related to the Sawari II and Pakistan submarine contracts.

It is hardly surprising that governments can become deeply involved in trying to ensure that defence companies win export contracts. After all, defence sales can make a major contribution to national security, technological advancement and job creation; they can play a role in forging closer relations with other countries; and, of course, they can generate enormous revenues – the global arms trade in 2017 was estimated to be worth at least US$95 billion,[11] and in 2018 France earned €6.97bn (US$8.23bn) from its sales of materiel.[12] But of course, arms-export policy reflects a balance between promotion and control. Based on a range of criteria, governments decide which types of equipment can be exported and which other countries are appropriate customers.

In France, politicians have tended to absolve themselves of responsibility for decisions regarding arms exports by relying instead on the efficacy of the government's bureaucratic machinery – and by using the bureaucracy as a lightning rod when questions arise about controversial sales. But when it comes to arms-export policy, it is illusory to pretend that a bureaucratic process, however rigorous, can somehow take the place of strategic political decision-making.

The choice facing France
There is a dilemma at the heart of France's armaments policy today: it wants to increase defence cooperation with its European

partners, in particular Germany, yet is reluctant to alter its liberal arms-export policy, which has been economically and strategically successful in the past. To explain how this contradiction came about, this book shows how the arms-export doctrine embedded itself in the French defence establishment and therefore became difficult to adapt. To understand the challenge the country faces, it is useful to consider:

- the origins, under President de Gaulle in the 1960s, of the doctrine of promoting arms exports;
- the bureaucratic institutional arrangements that continue to exert a powerful influence in favour of the status quo;
- the principal shifts in the global arms market since the end of the Cold War;
- the experimentation with placing greater restrictions on arms exports during President Chirac's years in office (1995–2007), followed by the reversion to the norm under President Nicolas Sarkozy (2007–12) and very few changes under his successor President Hollande (2012–17) or, so far, President Macron (2017–).

Put another way, this book considers the effects on French arms-export policy of rule by the right, the left and cohabitation, and suggests that the limited impact of differing stripes of government underlines the structural rigidities that are the embodiment of the long-standing doctrine. It will conclude with a look to the future and an exploration of potential avenues for change under President Macron, including the prospects for deeper cooperation with European partners in the field of arms-export policy.

CHAPTER ONE

The policy model for French arms exports

'We work on strictly commercial terms,' an adviser to Mr Debré says. 'We tell other countries: if you want arms, we sell them. It is all very simple.'[1]

1. Arms sales as the by-product of strategic autonomy

An independent arms industry serving an independent defence policy

When General Charles de Gaulle returned to power as president in May 1958, one of his objectives was to regain for France the independence and sovereignty that, in his view, his predecessors had compromised. Key tenets of de Gaulle's foreign policy were independence in decision-making, in particular from the United States, and the quest for *grandeur* (greatness) and *rang* (rank) on the international stage. *Grandeur* and independence went hand in hand, though they were not entirely synonymous. Independence meant being able to conduct foreign and defence policies that were not subject to constraints from other states, but *grandeur* also entailed seeking to influence international relations and break the logic of East–West confrontation. De Gaulle's foreign policy was thus centred on France having an active and independent role in international relations, and looking to increase its prestige.

The foundation of independence in defence, in de Gaulle's view, was nuclear weapons. The French nuclear doctrine was *tous azimuts*, a metaphor meaning 'in all directions', and it meant that no adversary was directly named – the Soviet Union was not clearly designated as the threat. The *tous azimuts* doctrine thus expressed a form of non-alignment, and above all allowed France to protect its territory without US assistance. However, producing nuclear weapons required a strong, autonomous and technologically advanced defence industry.

Under successive French governments, each of which subscribed to de Gaulle's vision, *grandeur* entailed the development of a strong and autonomous defence industry. Only by producing a full range of defence materiel for its armed forces – as well as nuclear weapons – could France avoid dependence on an external source of arms, namely the US. The defence industry therefore came to be seen a cornerstone of an independent defence policy and, in turn, a vital component of the country's strategic autonomy. This view of an independent defence industry as the guarantor of French independence lay at the heart of a consensus on defence policy that was accepted across the political spectrum.

The French state's main tool for developing an autonomous defence-industrial base was the Délégation ministérielle pour l'armement (DMA), part of the Ministry of Defence, which was created in April 1961 and is known today as the Direction générale de l'armement (DGA). The DMA held a pivotal position in French armaments policy as it purchased weapons from the defence industry, controlled and implemented defence-industrial policy, and was itself a weapons manufacturer.

Within the Ministry of Defence, the director of the DMA – a position first occupied by General Gaston Lavaud – was second only to the minister in terms of influence. The DMA was responsible for all issues relating to armaments, and initially had two main purposes: to develop an independent nuclear capability, and to procure conventional weapons to meet the needs of the French armed forces.

After the Second World War, the leaders of the Fourth Republic (1946–58) had begun to rebuild French defence-industrial capacity and lay the foundations for de Gaulle's later achievements in this field. Significant assistance came from the United States, which helped re-equip France's armed forces – for example in the post-war years the French Air Force bought US aircraft including the F-47 *Thunderbolt* – and contributed to the rebirth of the French defence industry by transferring manufacturing licences to French companies, which then produced main battle tanks and artillery systems based on American designs. After 1961 it was the DMA that look the lead in reshaping the French defence industry, through a consolida-tion process that created a number of large companies, each with a monopoly in its sector. Between 1952 and 1972, 40 enti-ties were converted, regrouped or closed.[2] The DMA allotted armaments programmes to the new companies; there was only a limited tendering process, and indeed very little competition in general.

The concentration and rationalisation process lasted through-out the Cold War. By the end of the 1980s a handful of defence manufacturers dominated each sector. Land-armaments production became a state monopoly, with companies and factories regrouped under the DMA's Direction technique des armements terrestres (DTAT) – later to become the Groupement industriel des armements terrestres (GIAT) and now known as Nexter. Naval production also became a virtual state monop-oly, under the DMA's Direction des constructions navales (DCN). The aerospace sector, meanwhile, underwent a dual process of consolidation and specialisation. The production of combat aircraft became the preserve of a private company,

Dassault (renamed Dassault Aviation in 1990), while production of helicopters and military transport aircraft was allotted to state-owned companies. In 1970 those state-owned companies were regrouped into a single entity, SNIAS, which was later renamed Aérospatiale and also took on responsibility for producing ballistic missiles.

By the end of the 1980s the only sectors where competition took place were tactical missiles and satellites (Aérospatiale and Matra), electronics (Thomson-CSF and Dassault Électronique) and military vehicles (GIAT Industries, Panhard and Renault Véhicules Industriels).

From autonomy to exports: forging a consensus in favour of arms sales

Throughout the Cold War the French narrative about *grandeur* and independence in defence policy developed in parallel with the defence industry itself, consolidating the foundations of the rationale for promoting arms exports.

The economic argument was essentially that France could not sustain a defence industry capable of fully equipping its own armed forces without massive sales abroad. Strategic independence was to be achieved through the domestic production of nuclear weapons, for which it was necessary to have autonomous capabilities in defence research and development (R&D) and in arms production. Though investment in the development of nuclear weapons implied a lower budget for conventional weapons, policymakers were nevertheless set on establishing a defence industry that could produce the full range of conventional equipment for the armed forces. This ambition could not be realised on the basis of the French defence market alone. Production runs for major weapons systems are relatively short, and the funds available for R&D are limited. But if the arms in question can also be exported, unit costs are lowered and there is more revenue available for reinvestment in innovative technologies.

France's desire for independence in defence policy, combined with inevitable budget constraints, forged what Edward Kolodziej called a 'chain of logic' that compelled the country to sell weapons widely abroad – *tous azimuts* – so as to maintain the productive capacity of its defence industry and not have to import arms itself.[3] Or to put it another way, arms exports played a vital role in ensuring that the French defence industry could meet the requirements of the country's own armed forces.

Arms exports were also regarded as benefiting the French economy as a whole, not only through their direct contribution to the balance of payments and job creation but also through spillover effects for civilian industry. This argument was habitually used by the defence industry and politicians, with the result that by the 1970s, as Kolodziej put it, 'any suggestion to cut arms sales abroad was perceived as tantamount to abandoning economic growth and modernization'.[4]

The doctrine that the government should promote arms exports emerged very clearly in French political discourse in the early years of the Fifth Republic (1958–). In 1961, for example, members of the Senate, the upper house of parliament, applauded the creation of an export-support department within the DMA, arguing that jobs were at stake and demanding improvements to other export-support mechanisms.[5] In 1967, a report submitted to the National Assembly, the lower house of parliament, strongly made the case that the defence industry depended on exports.[6]

Unsurprisingly, France's defence ministers also employed these economic arguments. Pierre Messmer (defence minister from 1960–69) declared in October 1966 that 'the prosperity of our aerospace industry depends essentially on exports'.[7] His successor Michel Debré (1969–73) was a strong proponent of arms sales, saying for example that exports were 'a question of the existence or non-existence of our arms industry. If it were restricted to the domestic market, it could not keep going, and there would no longer be any possibility of a truly national defence policy.'[8] The first Socialist defence minister during the Fifth Republic, Charles Hernu (1981–85), made a similar case in 1983: 'The additional contribution that foreign sales make to the activities of our arms industry is fundamental in order to ensure our country has an independent industry and to supply our armed forces at a sustainable cost for our economy.'[9] And this economic rationale is still powerful today: for example a 2014 study by McKinsey for the Ministry of Defence and the main defence-industry association (CIDEF) concluded that arms exports reduced France's trade deficit by 5–8% and sustained 40,000 jobs.[10]

The doctrine can also be seen, for example, in a letter sent in 1970 by defence minister Michel Debré to economy minister Valéry Giscard d'Estaing, in which he argued that a reduction in domestic arms procurement had obliged the defence industry to turn to foreign markets,[11] and in an internal Ministry of Defence memorandum sent in 1976, which stated that:

> A defence policy necessarily includes a policy of arms supply necessary for the armed forces. If we want a non-dependent defence policy … we are driven to maintain a significant national arms industry. But the arms industry is a cutting-edge industry, in which investment and R&D spending are high. If the industry were to satisfy only national needs, its prices would be prohibitive. Therefore we must widen the markets, through joint weapons development, offset agreements, and simple exports. … Conclusion: arms

exports in their broader sense are an imperative tied to the political will of our independent defence policy.[12]

The diplomatic or geopolitical component of the arms-export doctrine was rooted in the Gaullist belief that France should carve out its own niche, separate from the two super-powers, and that manufacturing its own arms was a means to attain greater independence from US influence. This logic could also be extended to other countries: if they armed them-selves independently, either by producing their own weapons or by buying from suppliers other than the US or the Soviet Union, this would help promote a multipolar rather than bipolar world. Therefore, the argument went, by selling arms to other countries France was enabling them to become more independent from the US or the Soviet Union.

This diplomatic argument, like the economic one, was evident in a variety of documents. The first defence white paper, written in 1972 when Debré was defence minister, described arms exports as a means of resisting the US–USSR duopoly: 'It is difficult to escape the duty to respond to certain countries' requests, when they are concerned about their own defence and want to secure it without having to ask for assis-tance from the dominant powers of the two blocs.'[13] Defence minister Yvon Bourges (1975–80) stated in 1975 that acquiring French arms gave countries the means to ensure their inde-pendence, emphasising that France did not attach political conditions to its arms sales or seek to interfere in other coun-tries' internal affairs.[14] In 1982, Hernu went somewhat further, declaring that 'France could, alongside the technical assis-tance it provides in terms of armaments, become the leader of the non-aligned countries'.[15] In 1984, an official in the DGA expressed the view that 'armaments can ... be part of a North–South dialogue which would, unlike our competitors, avoid ideological brainwashing'.[16] This argument was also used by successive prime ministers, whether from the political right or left, and echoed by the defence industry itself.[17]

This combination of economic and diplomatic justifications left little space for any counter-narrative in favour of restraining arms exports. The chain of logic had been forged and seemed impossible to break.

Creating the policy tools

With the economic and diplomatic justifications firmly in place, France embarked on a path of worldwide arms sales after the creation of the DMA in 1961. It proved to be a successful venture: in 1960 the country exported only 8% of the defence equipment it produced, but by 1990 the figure was 31%.[18]

In order to implement this policy, from the 1960s onwards the government set up an extensive political, bureaucratic and financial machinery. The most important instrument for promoting arms exports was the Direction des affaires internationales (DAI), a department within the DMA. The DAI was created in 1965 with the aim of boosting exports of aerospace and all military equipment. In the 1980s it became the Direction des relations internationales (DRI), and is today known as the Direction du développement international (DI).

Like its predecessors, the DI is involved in all government activities related to arms exports. For decades it has been responsible for establishing the overall national strategy; coordinating interministerial initiatives; maintaining contacts with foreign officials, with a view to opening new markets to French defence manufacturers; supervising exports by state-owned companies; overseeing the network of defence attachés working in French embassies around the world (until 2015, when this role was transferred to another department); organising arms fairs in France; coordinating financial assistance for the defence industry; participating in contract negotiations; and also offering an after-sales service that includes technical assistance for arms purchasers. Significantly, the DI also has an export-control role, as it participates in the process of assessing defence companies' applications for export licences.

After the predecessors to the DI, the most important instruments for French arms sales during the Cold War were a number of different export brokers or *Offices*, which were outside the administrative structure of the Ministry of Defence:

- SOFMA: Société française de matériels d'armement
- SOFRESA: Société française d'exportation de systèmes d'armement
- OGA: Office général de l'air
- OFEMA: Office français d'exportation de matériel aéronautique
- COFRAS: Compagnie française d'assistance spécialisée
- NAVFCO: Société navale française de formation et de conseil
- AIRCO: Société française de formation et de conseil aéronautique
- SOFREXAN: Société française d'exportation d'armement naval
- SOFREMAS: Société française d'exportation d'equipements et matériels spéciaux
- SOFEMI: Société française d'exportation du Ministère de l'Intérieur
- SOFRANTEM: Société française de vente de financements de matériels terrrestres et maritimes

Collectively, the *Offices* were a cornerstone of the export-promotion system – for example they were directly involved in about half of all French arms sales during the 1980s.[19] Some of the *Offices* were state-owned; others had mixed public and private ownership, with the government represented at board level via the DGA. Staffed mostly by former senior officers in the French armed forces, their mission was to promote French military equipment abroad (which included forging relationships with local officials), participate in negotiations and offer after-sales services. Most of these brokers were originally created to assist the state-run defence manufacturers GIAT and DCN in promoting their products and negotiating contracts abroad. GIAT and DCN were under the direct control of the DGA until the 1990s; as such they did not have their own in-house marketing departments, and indeed faced legal and administrative impediments in promoting their products. SOFMA and SOFRESA were linked to the state through exclusivity contracts for the sale of GIAT's and DCN's products, though other defence companies also benefited from the role the *Offices* performed.

There were also a series of instruments to provide French clients with attractive financial arrangements when buying French equipment. In particular, the Compagnie française d'assurance pour le commerce extérieur (COFACE), tied to the Ministry of the Economy until 1994, provided state guarantees, ensuring companies against the risk of non-payment. Through COFACE the state also secured credit provided by private banks to arms purchasers. More recently, since January 2017, this role has been taken up by Bpifrance, the French public investment bank.[20] The COFACE/Bpifrance guarantee benefits the arms buyer by making it unnecessary for them to immediately pay the French manufacturer the full price of their acquisition – instead they can repay the bank in instalments. Customers have to pay premiums for such services, as well as interest rates on the loans, which means that COFACE/Bpifrance fees can in fact become part of an attractive package for French arms exporters, if COFACE/Bpifrance offers them better terms than equivalent institutions in other countries. The state guarantee can also encourage commercial banks to offer more favourable loans for the customer, which in turn can help French defence firms in their negotiations.

Another subsidy for arms exports was the 'article 29' procedure, created in 1957, under which the state would pay for materiel that had been manufactured for export but not subsequently sold. There was also 'article 90', created in 1963 for aerospace equipment and extended to other materiel in 1968, under which a defence manufacturer that wanted to adapt a product to the specific needs of a foreign client could receive a government loan for that purpose, which was later repaid from sales proceeds. Article 29 no longer exists but article 90 is still in place.[21]

2. The dominance of arms-sales promoters in the decision-making process

The French system for arms-export control is interministerial in character, though it is the Ministry of Defence that exerts the strongest influence. When a defence firm wishes to sell weapons abroad, it applies to the Ministry of Defence for an export licence. The application will also be assessed by the Ministry of Foreign Affairs and the Ministry of the Economy, after which it will either be approved or rejected by an inter-ministerial process, the Commission interministérielle pour l'étude des exportations de matériels de guerre (CIEEMG). The CIEEMG's monthly meetings are chaired by the Secrétariat général de la défense et de la sécurité nationale (SGDSN). This process is conducted mainly by civil servants, but politically sensitive cases can be decided by the political staff in the prime minister's or the president's office – or even, occasionally, by the prime minister or the president themselves. A conspicuous

Figure 1.1. **The French system for arms-export control: bureaucratic and political actors**

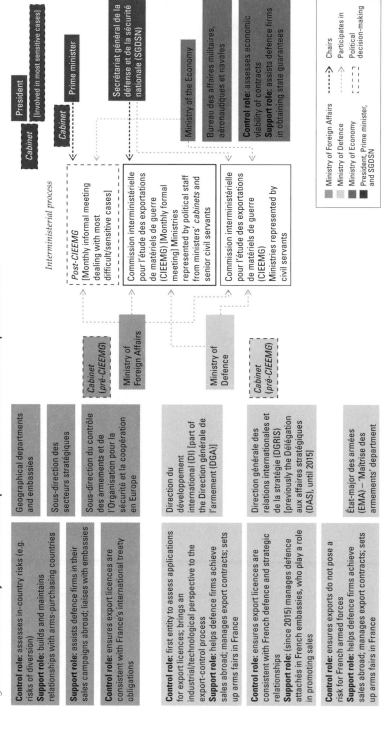

feature of the system – the importance of which cannot be over-stated – is that almost all of the entities with an export-control role are also involved in *promoting* exports (see Figure 1.1). Their dual role inevitably influences decisions about whether to grant export licences – and indeed has contributed, for almost 60 years, to the tilting of the system towards boosting rather than restraining sales of French arms.

The Ministry of Defence: tilting in favour of export promotion
Within the Ministry of Defence, three departments are involved in the export-control process: the DI, which is part of the DGA; the Délégation aux affaires stratégiques (DAS), renamed as the Direction générale des relations internationales et de la stratégie (DGRIS) in 2015; and the État-major des armées (EMA) or Defence Staff.

The DI is the most important example of an entity with the aforementioned dual role: its overarching mission is to help French defence companies promote and sell their products abroad, but it has an important position in the export-control process because it is the first department to receive and assess the companies' applications for export licences, after which it passes them on to the other ministries and departments involved in the CIEEMG process. An anecdote from a defence-industry executive illustrates this situation and gives an insider view of an instance when the DI used its position in the control process to help a company achieve an overseas sale:

> We had a problem with the political sub-department of the [Ministry of Foreign Affairs], which did not have the same opinion as the geographic sub-department and the ambassador, who both were in favour of the sale. I had to call [the DI's deputy director for export controls], who knew the director of the [Ministry of

Foreign Affairs'] political sub-department. We went to see him together. And the director said, 'Oh, so that's a problem for you? Well, in that case I can change [my position].[22]

The DI's dual role within the French arms-export system was also neatly encapsulated in a metaphor used by one of its former directors, Stéphane Reb:

Through the actions of the DGA and [the DI], the state is involved in both controlling and supporting defence exports, which allows it to subtly direct them by using the brakes or the accelerator according to the circumstances.[23]

The Defence Staff (EMA) have traditionally been more likely than the DI to restrict arms exports in certain cases. Their priorities when assessing defence companies' applications for export licences are 1) the need to maintain the credibility of France's nuclear deterrence (i.e. ensure that nuclear deterrence would not be compromised by the customer's acquisition of the product); 2) the security of the French armed forces on the battlefield (i.e. ensure there is no risk of the product subsequently being used against French personnel); and 3) security of supply (i.e. in the case of particularly sensitive equipment, ensure that all the suppliers potentially involved are French – so that, for example, French producers will not find themselves relying on foreign sub-contractors).[24] However, the EMA are another entity with the dual role of export control and promotion. They are involved in the export-control process through their 'arms control' department (Maîtrise des armements), which is itself subdivided into four parts including one, SOUTEX, which supervises the French armed forces' involvement in export campaigns.[25]

The third key player in the export-control system is the DGRIS (previously the DAS), which has a close relationship with the defence minister's political staff.[26] The DGRIS is also in charge of collecting the other Ministry of Defence departments' responses to export-licence applications. It oversees the ministry's diplomatic relationships and seeks to consolidate ties with arms-purchasing countries. It was particularly influential in the export-control process between 2000 and 2007, a period when there was a somewhat more restrained approach to arms sales.

Prior to the monthly interministerial CIEEMG meeting, representatives from the DI, EMA and DGRIS have a so-called *pré-CIEEMG* or *CIEEMG Défense* meeting, also attended by the political staff in the defence minister's *cabinet*, where they report to the official who advises the minister regarding arms sales, usually referred to as either the 'diplomatic adviser' or 'adviser for international affairs'. A previous occupant of this position explained how it too combined elements of export control and export promotion, memorably describing it as a role with 'a schizophrenic side'.[27]

If there is a disagreement between the three departments, the issue is dealt with by the minister's political staff. A former Ministry of Defence official recalled that in such cases the political staff could find themselves coming under pressure, with defence companies eager for their export licences to be granted but civil servants anxious to avoid any potential controversies.[28]

Within the system, the DI is perceived as prioritising high sales figures and defending the interests of the defence industry,[29] and owes its influence partly to the fact that it is the only entity within the Ministry of Defence that is staffed mostly by armaments engineers and therefore brings a unique technical expertise to the assessment of defence companies' applications for export licences. Also, as described by a Ministry of Defence official, the DGA and the minister's political staff themselves come under pressure to boost arms exports: 'The [annual arms-sales report submitted to parliament] tyrannises the DGA and the political staff, because they have to reach high numbers. There is a tyranny to get results.'[30] As for the DGRIS, the entity most directly concerned with arms-export-control issues, it lacks the means to act as a counterweight to the DGA: in 2018 it had a staff of only 210,[31] whereas the DGA contained around 10,000 civil servants.[32]

When the DGRIS was created in 2015 as the successor to the DAS, the new entity gained greater influence within the Ministry of Defence and also acquired new export-support responsibilities as it began supervising the global network of defence attachés in French embassies, whose work includes promoting sales of French materiel in the countries where they are posted. With DGRIS having taken on this role, it is now the case that all the Ministry of Defence departments involved in the export-control process also have, to varying degrees, an export-promotion function.

The Ministry of Foreign Affairs: conflicting interests

In the Ministry of Foreign Affairs (referred to colloquially as the 'Quai d'Orsay'), the decision-making process regarding arms exports also involves, from the earliest stages, actors whose role is essentially to promote sales. Three departments participate in the process: the Sous-direction du contrôle des armements et de l'Organisation pour la sécurité et la coopération en Europe, which is in charge of processing defence companies' applications for export licences when it receives them from the DI; the Mission du soutien aux secteurs stratégiques, in charge of export promotion; and the geographical departments (i.e. those covering specific regions of the world), which occasionally provide advice regarding export-licence applications.

Like the Ministry of Defence, the Ministry of Foreign Affairs has an internal consultation process that culminates in the political staff in the minister's *cabinet* issuing their opinion on whether an arms-export licence should be granted. The Sous-direction du contrôle des armements handles export-licence applications, and may ask a geographical department for additional advice. Anecdotal evidence from interviews suggests that the geographical departments want arms sales to go ahead in most cases.[33] As for France's ambassadors abroad, they too are in favour of arms sales 'nine times out of ten', according to a ministry official.[34]

Within the economic wing of the Quai d'Orsay, the role of the Sous-direction des secteurs stratégiques is to help French companies win export contracts. Its viewpoint carries weight when applications for export licences are being assessed. Indeed, according to a ministry official, 'the [Sous-direction] … is the pivot for the CIEEMG. The CIEEMG asks its opinion in case there are economic interests, or in case it's necessary to contact someone at the company to discuss the licence application.'[35] Another official explained that whereas staff from the Sous-direction des secteurs stratégiques participate in all the internal meetings – including the *pré-CIEEMG*, when the ministry's final position on any potential arms export is decided – the Sous-direction du contrôle des armements, in charge of assessing export-licence applications, is understaffed and simply does not have the capacity to become involved in the decision-making process to the same extent.[36]

The Ministry of the Economy: a marginal role
In the Ministry of the Economy (referred to colloquially as 'Bercy'), the only department involved in the control process for arms exports – the Bureau des affaires militaires, aéronautiques et navales – is also in charge of financing export

contracts. It is therefore yet another example of an actor with a foot in both the export-control and export-promotion camps, which makes it 'a bit schizophrenic' in the words of one of its officials.[37] In reality, the Ministry of the Economy is less important than either the defence or foreign ministry in the process of assessing and deciding on export licences – its main job, that of financing, takes place after a licence has been granted. One Bercy official described how the ministry's representatives always 'take the backseat'[38] during the CIEEMG meetings, while a former member of the defence minister's *cabinet* said bluntly that 'Bercy does not matter in the CIEEMG'.[39]

The SGDSN: at the head of the interministerial process

The other important administrative actor in the export-control process is the SGDSN, the defence and foreign-policy office of the prime minister. In this capacity, it officially represents the prime minister in the CIEEMG process. It is the only institution involved in the export-control process that does not also play a role, to some degree, in export promotion. It is the SGDSN that chairs, and therefore has the last word during, the monthly CIEEMG meetings. Most of the other actors regard it as taking a strict approach to arms-export controls, with one DGA official alleging that the 'SGDSN is paranoid … it has retained a mindset from the 1930s'.[40]

SGDSN civil servants feel strongly that their role is to protect the prime minister from political and judicial blame. In the words of one former SGDSN official:

> The service's mission, when there's a clear policy from the prime minister, is to implement it – and when there's no clear policy, it's to make sure the prime minister's political staff receive all the information they need, in the most objective manner. We have to

be careful not to make the prime minister sign something that violates France's international obligations.[41]

Furthermore, the SGDSN sees the CIEEMG process as guar-
anteeing its own institutional legitimacy. In its advisory role
for the prime minister on defence and foreign-policy matters,
the SGDSN faces competition from the defence and foreign
ministries – but on the subject of arms-export control it has
no bureaucratic rival. However, as will be seen below, those
who promote arms exports can outmuscle the SGDSN at a
later stage in the process, when the most sensitive cases are
discussed at a higher political level.

Representatives from the SGDSN and from the defence,
foreign and economy ministries come together once a month
during the full CIEEMG meeting. The first part of the proceed-
ings, typically lasting between an hour and an hour and a half,
is attended by the key decision-makers – political staff from
ministers' *cabinets*, the directors of the DI and DAS, the head of
the SGDSN – and typically deals with ten to 15 cases which are
problematic or sensitive and therefore need to be decided by
the more senior officials. Then, during the rest of the day, civil
servants typically take care of about 400 simpler cases, few of
which take more than a minute to decide.[42]

The CIEEMG meeting is the last step in a long administrative
process, and although it performs an important bureaucratic
function, its role should be kept in perspective. Particularly
with regard to the more lucrative or politically sensitive arms
deals, what the CIEEMG often does, in reality, is rubber-stamp
decisions that have already been taken at a higher level, rather
than exert any real influence itself. For example, in 2009, when
prime minister François Fillon announced that the French
government had just authorised the company DCNS to begin
discussions with Russia regarding the sale of *Mistral*-class

amphibious assault ships, it was taken for granted in the media that the CIEEMG would approve the decision.[43]

Therefore, although the SGDSN exercises restraint when it comes to arms-export decisions, and wields influence in the context of the CIEEMG meeting, the system as a whole is still weighted in favour of promotion rather than control.

The prime minister and the president: taking sensitive decisions

If the participants in the CIEEMG meeting do not agree with regard to a particular export-licence application, the issue is passed on to the office of the prime minister. Indeed, it is usual for the most economically important or diplomatically sensitive cases to be addressed at the *post-CIEEMG*, an informal meeting that takes place in the office of the prime minister with his political staff and sometimes – typically three or four times a year – the prime minister himself.[44]

The other attendees at the *post-CIEEMG* include political staff from the Ministry of Defence and Ministry of Foreign Affairs, and the directors of the DI, DAS and SGDSN.[45] It is significant that the SGDSN – the prime minister's defence and foreign-policy office – tends to find itself in a less comfortable position at the *post-CIEEMG* than at the CIEEMG itself, where it has procedural authority. Because the *post-CIEEMG* is essentially informal, all participants are able to express their opinions quite freely. It is a forum where, as vividly described by a former SGDSN civil servant, the SGDSN often finds itself pitched against defence- and foreign-ministry officials who are pushing for arms-export licences to be granted:

> We 'replay' a few [export-licence applications] from the CIEEMG in front of the prime minister's political staff, and we have to be quick. That's where I have to

be very careful to check if someone is lying or distort-
ing the facts, because it's hard to counter them quickly
and you need to convince the rest of the audience.[46]

As for the president, although representatives from his office
attend the CIEEMG meeting as observers,[47] he does not often
become personally involved in the process. But while the prime
minister retains formal responsibility for arms-export decisions,
political approval from the president is sometimes necessary. In
the words of a Ministry of Defence official, 'in the complicated
cases, or when it wants to cover its own back, the SGDSN goes
to the prime minister or to the Elysée directly'.[48] A politician
recalled that President Nicolas Sarkozy was keen to be involved:
'During the 2007–11 period, the DGA had direct contact with
the Elysée – it was the president who wanted to do everything.'[49]
And another politician provided the following summary:

> The president or the prime minister is involved in the
> decision if it is important. It is important for instance if the
> relationship with the country is essential, or problematic
> – a country that is not totally 'white' nor totally 'black'.
> Or if it's an export to let a company breathe. In such cases
> it's [the president] who decides, and quickly.[50]

Two recent examples of the head of state making the final
decision on French arms exports were both in the context of
Saudi Arabia's participation in the war in Yemen. President
François Hollande, in 2017, and President Emmanuel Macron,
in 2018, had to intervene to resolve disagreements about
whether to authorise further munitions sales to Riyadh between
the Ministry of Defence, which was in favour, and the Ministry
of Foreign Affairs, which was against. In both cases the presidential decision was to let the deal go ahead.[51]

3. French arms-sales policymaking: an unequal struggle

Indeed, the broader French political system is also tilted in favour of actors who generally seek to increase arms exports. Not only do defence firms have easier access to decision-makers in political institutions than anti-arms-trade non-governmental organisations (NGOs) do, but the prevailing doctrine on arms sales even stifles open debate on the issue.

Power asymmetries: defence firms versus NGOs

The French political and business elites are entwined through personal and professional networks that the country's *grandes écoles* play a significant role in creating. In the case of the defence industry, the Dassault family, for example, has had close ties with senior politicians for decades, and some Dassault family members have themselves been involved in politics. Marcel Dassault (1892–1986), who in 1929 founded the company now known as Dassault Aviation, was close to the presidents Giscard d'Estaing and Jacques Chirac.[52] His son Serge (1925–2018), the owner of the Dassault Group, was also a mayor, senator and the proprietor of one of France's leading newspapers, *Le Figaro*. Serge's son Olivier, a deputy in the National Assembly, was until recently involved in the Dassault Group in various capacities. The Lagardère family, which owned the missile firm Matra (later to become part of EADS/Airbus), also had close relationships with senior politicians, in particular President Chirac.[53]

The French state and the defence industry are also structurally close because they are interdependent, as indeed is the case in all arms-manufacturing countries. The French defence industry has long been seen as crucial for the country's strategic sovereignty, while of course the government is the defence industry's main customer. Indeed, as in many other countries, French defence manufacturers are in the privileged position of facing little competition in producing major weapons systems and selling them to the government.

A significant feature of this mutual dependency is the relationship between the defence industry and the DGA within the Ministry of Defence. As previously described, the DGA is a major player in French armaments policy, having acquired great authority on the basis of its technological competence and management expertise. This strong position allows it to impose its own procurement choices in most cases, and it has also gained significant autonomy in the management of weapons programmes.[54] Over the years, countless individuals working in the DGA and the defence industry have been connected by personal and professional ties that in many cases stemmed from a shared educational background at the École Polytechnique, a prestigious higher-education and research institution in the Paris suburbs, whose graduates include many of France's most senior military engineers.[55] The institution offers an excellent training in engineering, after which many of its graduates go into the civil service and reach senior positions in, for example, the DGA, the *cabinet* of the defence minister, or the Ministry of the Economy.[56] There is also a well-worn pathway from the civil service to senior positions in private companies, including in the defence industry – a revolving-door phenomenon known as *pantouflage*.

Close ties with the DGA have enabled the French defence industry to exert significant influence on defence-industrial policy and even, on occasion, persuade policymakers to change decisions that were not in line with the industry's preferences.[57] Connections between armaments engineers in government and those in the private sector have been seen to operate, for example, in the French aerospace sector,[58] in research institutions[59] and on the *Leclerc* tank programme.[60]

Meanwhile, there is comparatively little scope for civil-society organisations such as NGOs to influence policy. They might be invited to participate in consultation processes, but it is all too easy for their opinions subsequently to be disregarded. This can produce something of a vicious circle, with French civil-society organisations becoming enervated by their lack of participation in the political process and then finding it even more difficult to make their voices heard.

In France there are fewer NGO activists campaigning against the arms trade than in some other countries, such as the United Kingdom. The first voices raised on the issue were those of religious organisations, in the 1970s, who demanded that French swords should be converted into ploughshares. Successive governments paid them little attention, with Michel Debré (defence minister from 1969–73), for example, saying they showed a complete lack of understanding of defence issues.[61] It was not until the post-Cold War period that French anti-arms-trade NGOs became more organised, often coordinating with their counterparts in other countries. In the early 1990s various French NGOs (such as CCFD-Terre Solidaire and Centre de documentation et de recherche sur la paix et les conflits, later renamed as the Observatoire des armements), along with French affiliates of British NGOs such as Amnesty International and Oxfam, were either created or gained expertise. Some of them were involved in international campaigns such as the one against anti-personnel mines or in favour of a multilateral treaty regulating the trade in conventional weapons. But resources have always been very limited: during the period 2013–15, for example, CCFD[62] and the French affiliates of Amnesty International and Oxfam each only had one permanent member of staff working on arms-trade issues.

Such NGOs continue to face an uphill struggle in France because there is still very little public debate regarding the country's arms sales. In the words of a former deputy head of the DGA, Laurent Giovachini: 'Arms-trade issues rarely appear in public debate – the public are interested in the topic only sporadically.'[63] Or, as one DGA civil servant put it: 'In France, we don't have NGOs to bother us, unlike in the United Kingdom.'[64] This view was echoed by an NGO activist, who lamented that the arms-trade debate is 'unimportant' in France and that 'in the media you only see the sale of [combat aircraft] under a commercial headline – the issue of human rights, of development, is not raised'.

Indeed, over the years, the scandals involving French arms exports have generally not focused on the ethics of the transactions in themselves. For example, in the 1980s, when Ministry of Defence officials were found to have been complicit in secretly diverting artillery shells to Iran (*l'affaire Luchaire* – see Introduction), not only was there a lack of sustained public interest but also the media framed the story as one of corruption and political intrigue – there was conspicuously little discussion of whether it was justified for France to supply munitions to a theocratic regime that was in the midst of a war with Iraq. In the 1990s, a parliamentary inquiry into France's ambiguous role in the 1994 Rwandan genocide – there were suspicions that France had continued to supply the Rwandan government with weapons even after genocide had begun – did not precipitate a significant debate about French arms sales, as the ensuing report not only concluded that France bore no responsibility for the genocide but also avoided any judgement regarding the government's arms-export policy.[65] Much more recently, in the 'Kazakhgate' affair concerning France's sale of military helicopters to Kazakhstan in 2010, when Sarkozy was president, public and media interest focused not on the ethics of supplying materiel to an authoritarian regime but on possible kickbacks and whether Sarkozy had facilitated the deal by pressuring Belgium to release from custody two Kazakh businessmen who were facing corruption charges.[66]

The limited role of parliament

A significant feature of French foreign and defence policy-making – including the decision-making process regarding arms exports – is the very limited power of parliament. Under the Fifth Republic, due both to the institutional framework and the way French politics works in practice, foreign and defence policy have become the *domaine réservé* of the president, who has acquired the power to take decisions single-handedly.[67] It is the president, for example, who would decide whether to use the country's nuclear deterrent. The president can also send French forces to fight overseas without parliament's prior authorisation, although since 2008 parliament has had the power to vote on whether to prolong any foreign military operation after it has been under way for four months. More recently, since the July 2016 terrorist attack in Nice, it is interesting to note that the Elysée has hosted weekly meetings of the Conseil de defense et de sécurité nationale (CDSN).[68]

Furthermore, it is noticeable in both the National Assembly and the Senate that many of the parliamentarians who take the greatest interest in defence-related issues are those with defence manufacturers or military garrisons in their constituencies.[69] Indeed, according to an NGO activist, there are only three categories of French parliamentarian who become involved in arms-export issues:

> Those who have military garrisons or defence firms in their constituencies – they protect jobs and are friends with the local CEOs, who then set up support committees for their re-election. Then the Communists, who want disarmament. Then those who have had careers

as military officers, or who have a special interest in these issues. … Also, on the defence committee there are deputies who didn't get a seat [on any other committee], and so they find themselves there but they're not interested in the discussions.[70]

The pre-eminence of the executive on defence issues also seems to generate a certain reticence on the part of parliamentarians, who are often prone to adopt the attitude that decisions on defence policy should be taken elsewhere. For example, in annual budget discussions, the deputies in the National Assembly take the view that it is not their role to seek to change the government's proposal for the budget of the Ministry of Defence – instead they merely supervise the budget's implementation. As one deputy put it, 'we do not ask for co-decision with the government in this field'.[71]

Parliament is particularly weak when it comes to scrutinising the government's arms-export policy. The only analytical tool made available to parliamentarians is the annual report produced by the DGA, detailing the contracts signed and export licences granted during the previous year. Also, parliamentarians have failed to make good use of the information at their disposal. An NGO employee recalled that during President Sarkozy's time in office, 'NGOs had to remind the deputies that there was a report for parliament. They don't use the report. They don't do their job on this issue.' The defence minister between 2012 and 2017, Jean-Yves Le Drian, took the initiative of going in person to present the annual arms-export report to the members of the defence and foreign-affairs committees of the National Assembly and Senate. The second time he did so, in September 2013, he found himself addressing a very sparse audience. He declared that he had come 'to honour a commitment that I made to you … I insisted on presenting [the report], even if it's not an overwhelming success. But as my grand-mother would say, only the best of us are here.'[72] According to another politician, it is simply the case that 'few parliamentar-ians are interested in defence issues – it's too complicated',[73] while a civil servant in the Ministry of Defence described the situation in the bluntest terms: French parliamentarians 'don't give a damn' about controlling arms exports, he said.[74]

Political parties and arms-export policy choices

Not only does parliament have a limited role within the arms-export policymaking framework, but the parliamentarians who do advocate a more restrained approach to arms sales have tended to find themselves in a weak position.

In French defence and foreign policy, one inheritance from the de Gaulle era is that all the main political parties uphold the doctrine of supporting arms exports. The main three political parties in France today are Les Républicains (LR), previously known as the Union pour un Mouvement Populaire (UMP), on the right; the Parti socialiste (PS), on the left; and the new, centrist party currently in power, La République En Marche (LREM), which was created by Emmanuel Macron in 2016 before he became president the following year.

During his successful campaign for the presidency in 2012, the PS candidate François Hollande stated in an article in the *Revue Défense Nationale* that he wanted 'a strong, coherent and controlled defence industry'. The importance of the control element, he wrote, 'justifies that the government reports annu-ally to parliament on its [arms-sales] choices. To a renewed transparency effort we will add more efficient control mecha-nisms regarding equipment, intermediaries and end-users.'[75] This implied that Hollande might have been lending a favour-able ear to the arguments of NGOs – an impression that did not last long when he became president (see Chapter Five). Five years later, in 2017, the PS presidential candidate was Benoît Hamon, generally considered more left-wing than Hollande. However, he made no public commitment to limiting arms sales; he merely said that environmental standards should be applied to arms manufacturing, which among other benefits would make the products 'more autonomous and therefore more attractive for export'.[76]

In his successful 2017 presidential campaign, Macron did not state any position on arms sales, apart from praising 'export successes' in an interview with the *Revue Défense Nationale*.[77] However, there were already indications, including leaked emails that surfaced via WikiLeaks,[78] that he would continue the liberal arms-export policy. After more than two and a half years in power, his government has shown no sign of questioning the traditional doctrine. One former LREM deputy, Sébastien Nadot, who has since left the party, called in April 2018 for a full parliamentary inquiry into French arms sales to Saudi Arabia in the context of the war in Yemen[79] – but the party and its allies in the National Assembly blocked the move by authorising only a fact-finding mission, which had less investigative power.[80]

The current government's former spokesperson, Benjamin Griveaux, and the leader of LREM in the National Assembly, Richard Ferrand, have dismissed challenges to French arms sales.[81] President Macron's liberal policy on arms exports – in particular sales to Saudi Arabia and the United Arab Emirates (UAE) against the backdrop of the Yemen conflict – has led to a rift with the German government, which favours a stricter approach. The starkest example of this recent discord came after Chancellor Angela Merkel announced an embargo on arms sales to Saudi Arabia following the murder of Saudi journalist Jamal Khashoggi, which led Macron to accuse her of 'demagoguery' in October 2018.[82]

The only French political parties that have consistently advocated stricter controls on arms exports are two smaller ones: Europe Écologie Les Verts (EELV) and the Parti communiste français (PCF). In their 2012 manifesto, for example, EELV argued that there should be tighter controls and greater transparency, and also that the European Union should 'regulate' and 'moralise' the armaments sector.[83] Also in 2012, the leftist presidential candidate Jean-Luc Mélenchon promised Amnesty International that he would achieve 'better control of arms exports' if elected.[84] In 2017 Mélenchon ran again – this time for a new left-wing party, La France insoumise – and his manifesto denounced France's participation in the 'exports race' as being against the 'principles and interests' of the Republic, with particular reference to arms sales in the 'Middle East' and to the 'Gulf monarchies'.[85]

As for the far-right Rassemblement National (RN), formerly the Front National (FN), it has never been in a position to exert much influence over France's defence or foreign policies. But the perspective of its leader Marine Le Pen, who reached the second round of the 2017 presidential election, is clear: in her manifesto she insisted that arms exports could be increased and used more effectively as a diplomatic tool.[86]

OVERVIEW: The 'golden age' of French arms exports, 1960–85

In 1967, when President de Gaulle imposed an arms embargo on the countries involved in the Six-Day War, the measure was seen primarily as a rebuke to Israel, a major buyer of French materiel until then, and therefore made Arab countries more receptive towards French arms exports. Also, because of decolonisation in the 1960s, there were many newly independent countries that needed to equip their armed forces and in many cases did not want to rely primarily on either the United States or the Soviet Union for their arms purchases. The difficulty of penetrating the markets of NATO or other Western-aligned countries, which tended to favour the US as their arms supplier, was another reason why the French defence industry established strong relationships with developing-world customers in this period.

Major sales, 1960–85

Iraq: 30 *Mirage* F-1E fighter/ground-attack (FGA) aircraft, ordered 1977, delivered 1980–82; 59 *Mirage* F-1E FGA aircraft, ord. 1979, del. 1982–85

Libya: 78 *Mirage*-5D FGA aircraft, ord. 1970, del. 1971–73; 32 *Mirage*-5DE FGA aircraft, ord. 1970, del. 1973–74

South Africa: 3 *Daphné* submarines, ord. 1968, del. 1970–71; 32 *Mirage* F-1A FGA aircraft, ord. 1971, del. 1976–77; 16 *Mirage* F-1C FGA aircraft, ord. 1971, del. 1975–76

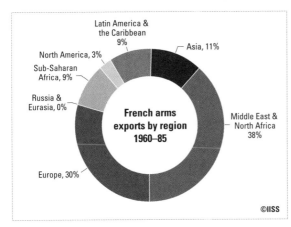

Top ten customers, 1960–85:

1. Iraq
2. Germany
3. Spain
4. Libya
5. Saudi Arabia
6. South Africa
7. Pakistan
8. Egypt
9. Morocco
10. Belgium

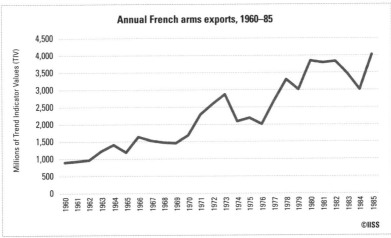

Source for all data: SIPRI Arms Transfers Database

CHAPTER TWO

The new post-Cold War arms market: competition, regulation and Europeanisation

The evolution of the European and global arms market has inevitably had an impact on French arms-export policy. The defence industry experienced a severe slump after the end of the Cold War, as total worldwide military spending fell dramatically. The global trade in arms, which had already been slowing during the 1980s, continued its downward trajectory for the first half of the 1990s. Internationally, including at the European level, the post-Cold War period also saw the emergence of initiatives to better regulate global arms transfers, and the linking of human-rights issues to the arms trade. Overall, this profoundly changed the context in which France formulated its arms-export policy.

1. Challenging times for the arms industry

Ups and downs in global demand for arms

Three different phases can be distinguished in the post-Cold War period: 1990–2000, which saw a continued contraction in the global arms trade; 2000–08, when the trade started to expand again; and then another contraction in the wake of the 2008 financial crisis, which it took a decade to recover from.

With the demise of the Soviet Union having removed the primary justification for high levels of Western military expenditure, the defence budgets of NATO countries decreased sharply in the 1990s (Figure 2.1).

The global arms trade had already begun to decelerate in the early 1980s as a result of lower oil prices, which reduced Middle Eastern countries' defence budgets, and the end of procurement cycles in many arms-importing countries. So when military spending fell sharply in North America and Europe a few years later, the overall impact on the global arms market was dramatic. Several major Western importers cancelled important procurement programmes planned since the 1980s, which further contributed to the decrease in international arms transfers (Figure 2.2).[1]

With the exception of a brief surge in 1992, it was only in the second half of the 1990s that global military expenditure returned to an upwards trajectory. The strong growth after the turn of the millennium was driven partly by US defence spending, which accelerated in the wake of 9/11 not only because of the wars in Afghanistan and Iraq but also the drive to modernise the US armed forces by incorporating new technology. Military spending also rose elsewhere in the world, notably in the so-called BRIC countries – Brazil, Russia, India and China – and indeed in Asia as a whole (Figure 2.3).

Following the return to growth in global military expenditure, the global arms trade also began to expand again from 2003 (Figure 2.2). But the 2008–09 financial crisis, particularly its subsequent impact on government finances in Western countries, brought this expansion to a halt. The fact that US and European governments needed to limit public spending, combined with the scaling down of the military operations in

Figure 2.1. **Annual military expenditure in North America and Western Europe, in constant (2016) US$m, 1970–2017**

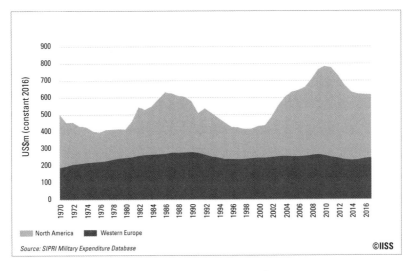

Source: SIPRI Military Expenditure Database ©IISS

Figure 2.2. **Annual global arms transfers, 1975–2018[2]**

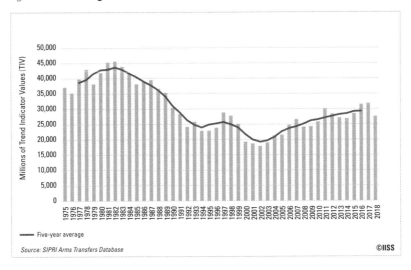

Source: SIPRI Arms Transfers Database ©IISS

Iraq and Afghanistan, pushed down Western defence spending from the late 2000s. But in the rest of the world, defence spending continued to edge upwards (Figure 2.3). This divergence between the West and the rest of the world (apart from sub-Saharan Africa) has changed the dynamics of the global arms trade, with sales flowing increasingly towards Asia and the

Figure 2.3. **Military expenditure per region, in constant (2016) US$m, 1988–2017**[3]

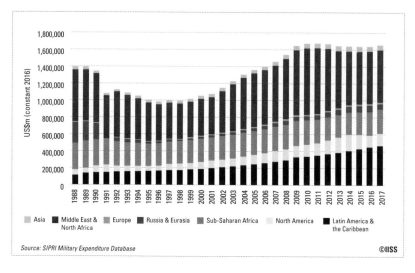

Source: SIPRI Military Expenditure Database ©IISS

Figure 2.4. **World arms imports per region, 1975–2018**[4]

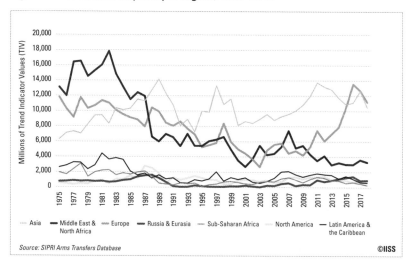

Source: SIPRI Arms Transfers Database ©IISS

Middle East after 2000 (Figure 2.4). From the perspective of the defence industries in European countries, therefore, foreign markets became increasingly attractive.

But in the West in the last couple of years, military expenditure has been increasing again as a result of rising tensions in many parts of the world – for example because of Russia's invasion of Crimea and subversion in eastern parts of Ukraine – and also American pressure for its European NATO partners to make a greater financial contribution.[5]

Supply trends: the advent of a buyers' market

From the 1990s onwards, as a result of these shifting regional dynamics, American and European defence firms found themselves facing increased competition for arms contracts, with the emergence of new defence suppliers such as Israel, Turkey, South Korea, Brazil and China. China, in fact, rose to become the world's third-largest arms exporter in the period 2011–15, overtaking Germany, France and the UK.[6] Now that they were able to choose between a greater number of suppliers, arms-purchasing governments found themselves in a stronger negotiating situation – which they exploited, for example, by insisting that technology transfers should be included in arms deals, so as to help them develop their own defence industries.

Another development in the mid-2000s was that arms-purchasing countries became more sophisticated in their offset policies (i.e. provisions that countries attach to their purchases of defence equipment from foreign suppliers, usually in order to receive some form of economic benefit in return). This was particularly true of the Gulf states, where arms-procurement processes changed dramatically. Between the 1970s and the 1990s, as Emma Soubrier has shown, the main goal of Gulf states' arms imports was more diplomatic than military: they were a means of forging closer ties with Western arms-exporting countries. The Gulf states did not explicitly define their own military requirements, so Western firms and governments could impose their own interests. Furthermore, given their limited capabilities in terms of industrial production, the Gulf states imported materiel 'off the shelf', with nothing or very little in the way of technology transfers. Since the mid-2000s, however, they have strengthened their acquisition processes. Nowadays they include operational and capacity criteria in their procurement choices, and are more likely to request technology transfers because their industrial capacity has improved – notably in the case of the United Arab Emirates.[7]

2. A multilateral agenda for arms-export controls: emerging regulations

Alongside these economic trends, diplomatic developments after the Gulf War (1990–91) pushed the issue of arms-trade control to the heart of multilateral negotiations. This prompted a number of international initiatives aimed at achieving better cooperation between states on the issue of arms exports.

Arms-trade control rises up the multilateral agenda

The Gulf War brought American and other Western armed forces face to face with an adversary that had been equipped with a range of Western-manufactured equipment. In fact, the countries comprising the coalition against Saddam Hussein had provided 22% of the arms imported by Iraq in the period 1981–90.[8] This raised awareness in the US and among European arms exporters – particularly the UK and Germany – about the risks arising from an insufficiently regulated arms trade.

A number of initiatives were then taken to ensure better oversight of the arms trade. In March 1991, US president George H.W. Bush declared that it was necessary to 'act to control the proliferation of weapons of mass destruction and the missiles used to deliver them'.[9] In June 1991, French president François Mitterrand announced a 'disarmament plan' that included the objective of creating a United Nations office dedicated to promoting disarmament efforts (achieved in 1998 in the form of the UN Department for Disarmament Affairs).[10] Also in June 1991, the European Council in Luxembourg adopted a Declaration on Non-Proliferation and Arms Exports, which included criteria for assessing applications for arms-export licences. In July 1991, G7 governments adopted a Declaration on Conventional Arms Transfers and NBC Non-Proliferation. In October 1991 the permanent members of the UN Security Council agreed on common guidelines to regulate arms transfers. In November 1993, the Conference on Security and Co-operation in Europe (later to become the Organization for Security and Co-operation in Europe – OSCE) agreed on the 'principles and guidelines governing conventional arms transfers'.[11] Even though most of these initiatives had no immediate impact on national policies, they paved the way for later multilateral agreements on arms-export controls.

Besides the Gulf War, various other factors in the 1990s led towards the adoption of humanitarian norms by participants in the arms trade. A growing number of civil wars, including ethnic conflicts, showed the possible consequences of unchecked flows of small arms and light weapons. Furthermore, the increasing influence of non-governmental organisations (NGOs) was a key factor in explaining the arrival of arms-export controls on the multilateral political agenda. Pressure from an international coalition of hundreds of NGOs was key in achieving the Ottawa Treaty (1997), which aimed to ban the production and sale of anti-personnel mines – a normative shift in the sense that it established a clear connection between the arms trade and human-rights issues. This was followed in 2008 by the Oslo Convention on cluster munitions. While these were treaties banning specific types of weapons, rather than regimes for regulating the arms trade in a broader sense, they nonetheless had the effect of energising the NGOs and inspiring the international campaign that helped bring about the most significant attempt to regulate the international trade in conventional weapons – the Arms Trade Treaty (ATT), which was adopted by the UN General Assembly in 2013 and entered into force in 2014.

Another means of exerting greater control over the arms trade was through increased transparency. From the early 1990s, the governments of arms-exporting countries began making information available about how much materiel they were selling and who was buying it. In December 1991, in the wake of the Gulf War, the United Nations Register of Conventional Arms (UNROCA) was established, with the aim that every country would voluntarily produce annual reports on their exports and imports of seven categories of materiel,[12] and then submit the reports to the UN. Although the rate of reporting has dropped in the last decade,[13] UNROCA was helpful in providing an initial impetus towards greater transparency.

France began publishing a comprehensive report on arms exports in 2000, as did Germany. By 2001, both countries' reports, and also that of the United Kingdom, included information on small arms and light weapons, in addition to the other UNROCA categories.[14] South Africa began to divulge its arms exports in 2005, followed in 2009 by five of the Balkan countries – Albania, Bosnia-Herzegovina, Macedonia, Montenegro and Serbia. Croatia and Hungary published their first reports in 2010, and Poland in 2011.

Other multilateral and bilateral influences on European arms-export controls

In addition to the new international agreements aimed at better regulating the arms trade, French and other European defence manufacturers faced other multilateral and bilateral constraints on their export policies from the 1990s onwards.

During the Cold War, a multilateral regime composed mainly of NATO members, the Coordinating Committee for

Multilateral Export Controls (CoCom), controlled transfers of arms and dual-use goods to the Eastern Bloc. It was dismantled in November 1993 and replaced in December 1995 by the Wassenaar Arrangement (WA), which became operational in July 1996. States party to the WA agree on common export-control lists and on how to control non-listed items, verify end-users and monitor emerging technologies that could become sensitive. They also maintain lists of conventional arms (Munitions List) and dual-use goods and technologies (Dual-Use List), which are reviewed annually. These lists are regularly included into EU law in a directive for defence products, and in a regulation for dual-use goods.

Other arrangements focus specifically on certain types of goods and technologies. The Nuclear Suppliers Group's Non-Proliferation Principle (1994) aims to limit exports of nuclear equipment, materials or technology; the Australia Group (1985) focuses on controlling exports of items that could be used to produce chemical or biological weapons; and states participating in the Missile Technology Control Regime (MTCR) (1992) seek to tightly control exports of items used in the development of 'unmanned delivery systems' (i.e. missiles and uninhabited aerial vehicles) capable of delivering weapons of mass destruction. Arms-exporting states have all had to take into account these multilateral rules, which multiplied after the end of the Cold War.

Over the years, as the internationalisation of the arms industry has created an interdependence between defence firms in different countries, and therefore between governments, many Western arms-exporting countries have been subjected to pressure from one other country in particular – the United States. The US is involved in a large proportion of international arms-production processes, and some of its arms-export regulations – specifically the International Traffic in Arms Regulations

(ITAR) – have extraterritorial application. The ITAR rules cover products that contain US components or are designed using US technical data. They apply to the product whatever its final destination, and for its entire life cycle.[15] Because of the ITAR's extraterritoriality, many states and companies must comply with US law. But the US also has additional means to influence other states' arms-export controls. In 2000 the Clinton administration launched the 'Defence Trade Security Initiative', intended to facilitate trade in defence products with allies such as the UK and Australia, but Washington required in exchange a 'Declaration of Principles'[16] through which prospective trading partners had to harmonise their export-control regulations with those of the US.

Washington began to adopt a more cautious approach towards export controls in the early 2000s – a change in attitude reflected, according to French officials, by increased US interference. Under the Wassenaar Arrangement the US had promoted a more liberal vision of defence trade in the immediate post-Cold War era, but after 9/11 the American government tried to use the WA to prevent weapons of mass destruction proliferating and, in particular, falling into the hands of terrorists. An official in France's Ministry of Defence described how, in the wake of 9/11, the US started to enforce its own ITAR regulations more rigorously, reclassify certain products and strengthen administrative procedures – for example, in its dealings with France, by insisting that the officials signing re-export certificates should have a certain level of seniority. Sometimes the French would simply refuse to comply.[17] But in general, according to a French defence-industry executive, European companies tended to follow this US-led trend towards strengthening arms-export controls, adopting a more cautious approach so as to ensure they could continue doing business in the US market.[18]

Today, the issue of US extraterritorial controls through the ITAR regulations has become a key concern for French defence policymakers and arms manufacturers. For example, it seems that the US vetoed a French sale of satellite components to the United Arab Emirates in 2013, and of SCALP missile components to Egypt in 2018 (which consequently obstructed the sale of *Rafale* combat aircraft to Cairo).[19] As a consequence, so as to avoid any repeat of such situations, there are ongoing efforts in France to develop 'ITAR-free' weapons sub-components.[20] The company MBDA, for instance, has invested in research and development, and acquired a number of innovative smaller companies to help it steer that path.[21] The Direction générale de l'armement (DGA) is also showing an interest in French start-ups that manufacture components that could be incorporated into French weapons systems.[22]

3. In search of a common defence market: towards Europeanisation

The impact of the post-Cold War changes was particularly significant in Europe, where the economic challenges facing the defence industry led to privatisations, restructuring and internationalisation. In the aerospace and electronics sectors across Europe, two main transnational champions emerged: Thales, the result of a merger between French firm Thomson-CSF and British company Racal; and EADS (today Airbus Group), the result of a merger between Aérospatiale (France), CASA (Spain) and the aerospace operations of DASA (Germany). Today, the defence market in most European countries is dominated by a few big groups who produce weapons systems across different sectors, such as BAE Systems in the UK and Saab in Sweden. Restructuring also led to internationalisation, with some of the biggest companies, such as Thales, creating or acquiring production and administrative facilities in more than country.

These industrial transformations created a need for greater integration between European defence markets and increased European cooperation, and led to reforms of arms-export control at the European level.

The Letter of Intent and the Farnborough Framework Agreement

In July 1998, six European countries – France, Germany, Italy, Spain, Sweden and the UK – launched a Letter of Intent (LoI), a process intended to foster direct, intergovernmental armaments cooperation outside the institutions of the EU. The LoI was subsequently formalised by the Farnborough Framework Agreement in July 2000.[23] The six countries, which in the 1990s accounted for about 90% of arms production in the EU, wanted to reduce the obstacles facing the trans-European defence groups that were then emerging, and to take steps towards creating a single European defence market. The idea came originally from European defence companies that wanted governments to reduce the disparities between the regulations in different countries, and one of the specific objectives of the LoI was to simplify the movement of defence products between the signatory states. While the LoI did not only deal with export controls, according to a Swedish diplomat 'the original reason for the Letter of Intent was export control'.[24] The Farnborough Framework Agreement dealt with six issues: security of supply; export provisions; security of information; research and technology; treatment of technical information; and harmonisation of military requirements. 'Export provisions' included cooperation between the LoI countries on exports of jointly developed weapons systems to other countries, as well as intra-LoI exports. Regarding exports of joint programmes, the LoI countries agreed on 'white lists' of countries to which sales could be authorised. However, if one of the

LoI signatories thought the recipient country was behaving in a way that threatened regional or international peace, or that its internal situation (in terms of civil conflict or human-rights abuses) had deteriorated significantly, it could initiate a moratorium on sales to that country and potentially, in consultation with the other signatories, have it removed from the list.[25]

Under the Farnborough Framework Agreement, France, Germany, Italy, Spain, Sweden and the UK arranged to simplify licensing procedures for defence products that formed part of joint programmes or would be used by the armed forces of one of those countries. This was to be implemented through global project licences (GPLs), replacing the individual licences that had previously been needed every time that a defence product was transferred between two LoI countries.[26]

The EU Code of Conduct and Common Position

While the LoI was an intergovernmental process, efforts to harmonise arms-export controls were also taking place at the EU level, culminating in the Code of Conduct on arms exports adopted on 8 June 1998 by the Council of the European Union.[27] The code endorsed eight criteria that EU member states would then consider when assessing export-licence applications from defence manufacturers, and stipulated that if an application did not comply with one of the eight criteria, the licence should be refused. The criteria included 'respect for human rights' and whether there were 'tensions or conflicts' in the country of final destination, the preservation of regional stability, and the risk of diversion.[28] The Code of Conduct also established a notification system that obliged the government of any EU country to notify all the others if it had refused to issue an export licence. If another member state later wished to grant a licence for an 'essentially identical transaction', it was obliged to consult with the country that had earlier refused to do so, and to justify its decision.[29] This was intended to dissuade countries from stepping in to seal an arms deal that another country had refused on the basis of the Code of Conduct's criteria – so-called 'undercutting'. In this way the Code of Conduct was therefore not only a way to establish human-rights norms but also to prevent unfair competition between the EU's arms-exporting members. Although there are still differences between the ways in which member states have implemented the Code of Conduct's criteria, this was nevertheless a step forward in terms of European cooperation.

The foundations for the Code of Conduct had been put in place in 1991–92, after the Gulf War. In June 1991, seven criteria for arms-export control were agreed at the European Council's meeting in Luxembourg, with an eighth added in Lisbon a year later. The European Parliament, meanwhile, adopted three resolutions calling for stricter export controls (September 1992, March 1994 and January 1995). However, between 1992 and 1997, the French and British governments took the view that arms-export policy should not be dealt with at the EU level.[30]

Until the 1990s the major European arms exporters – including France – had been reluctant to cooperate on arms-export control, so why did they begin to change position? There were a number of different motives, in fact, that converged to produce the 1998 Code of Conduct.

Firstly, the harmonisation of European export controls was in the interests of the governments and defence industries themselves. The emergence of trans-European companies, with Europe-wide supply chains and cross-border joint ventures, created new needs with regard to export control. These companies had to devote time and resources to ensuring they complied with different sets of national rules – a handicap their American competitors did not face. It would clearly benefit them if defence products could circulate more easily within Europe. Another problem was the uncertainty defence manufacturers faced when exporting to countries outside the EU: to do so they required the assent of all the countries involved in the production process, so in this sense too the prospect of harmonisation was attractive. Moreover, European decision-makers began to fear that, because of the differences between countries' export-control regulations, firms would seek to locate some of their manufacturing operations to countries with less restrictive rules – so-called 'licence shopping'.

Secondly, demands for common export-control rules were also coming from civil society. British NGOs in particular – such as Saferworld, Amnesty International, Oxfam, Campaign Against the Arms Trade (CAAT) and the International Action Network on Small Arms (IANSA) – campaigned from the early 1990s for tighter restrictions on arms exports and succeeded in influencing the Labour Party, whose manifesto during its successful 1997 general-election campaign, under Tony Blair, declared a commitment to 'supporting an EU code of conduct on arms sales, while maintaining ... support for a strong UK defence industry and defence through NATO'.[31] When Labour took power it pushed for an EU-wide initiative on arms-export controls. By this time NGOs all over Europe, supported by their British counterparts, were demanding that governments take human-rights issues into account when deciding on arms sales.

Therefore, by the late 1990s, the interests of European governments, defence industries and NGOs were converging on the adoption of common criteria for the control of arms exports. However, after the Code of Conduct was adopted in 1998, some NGOs argued that it did not go far enough and was being interpreted too liberally, so they began demanding a stricter code. Moreover, because the Code of Conduct was not legally binding, the Court of Justice of the European Union could not punish states that did not comply with it.

Table 2.1. **Arms exports to China (value of licences issued, in US$m) 2003–10**[33]

	2003	2004	2005	2006	2007	2008	2009	2010
France	119.2	213.2	210.2	188.6	344.7	284.3	31.8	263.6
Germany	--	1.4	1.1	0.1	3.6	6.0	0.1	1.5
UK	89.9	139.9	183.7	110.6	42.4	16.6	36.4	9.3

Source: European Union, European External Action Service – annual reports on arms exports

In 2000, EU member states began to discuss the possibility of making the Code of Conduct legally binding, through the Working Party on Conventional Arms Exports (COARM).[32] When a formal evaluation of the code began in 2003, NGOs stepped up their campaigns. Again it was the British NGOs that were particularly active, taking the leading role in pressing the EU to replace the Code of Conduct with a legally binding Common Position, a draft version of which was issued in June 2005. However, there was opposition to this move – and it came mainly from France.

The French government refused to support the creation of a Common Position unless the EU arms embargo against China, adopted in June 1989 after the Tiananmen Square massacre, was lifted in exchange. Because the embargo was not legally binding, it was open to varying interpretations – and it is worth noting that in the years when the lifting of the embargo was being debated (2003–05, principally), France exported far more defence equipment to China than Germany and the UK, the biggest of the EU's other major arms suppliers (Table 2.1). Those French exports mainly comprised imaging and countermeasures equipment, aircraft equipment and electronic equipment.

Nonetheless, France still considered the embargo too restrictive, and French officials saw the debate on the EU Code of Conduct as an opportunity to get it lifted. Initially, in fact, France led a group of countries that were all opposed to the embargo.[34] From 2006 onwards France was the only EU country that continued to oppose the upgrading of the Code of Conduct, but it was still able to stall the move because the adoption of the Common Position required a consensus.[35]

The 2009 defence package: the movement of defence products within the EU

While NGOs were pressing the EU to adopt the Common Position, the European Commission (EC) was aiming to simplify intra-EU regulations for trade in defence products because the results of the LoI process had been disappointing, as will be seen in Chapter Four. But EU member states were initially reluctant to embrace the commission's initiatives.

Since the mid-1990s the EC had become increasingly involved in defence-industrial issues, for example with its 1996 communication on 'The challenges facing the European defence-related industry – a contribution for action at European level',[36] and in 1997 on 'Implementing European Union strategy on defence-related industries'.[37] The latter contained a plan to simplify rules for the movement of defence products within the EU, but member states did not follow up on the proposal.

As early as 1995 there had been discussions in the Working Group on European Armaments Policy (POLARM) about simplifying the intra-EU arms trade, but they did not produce substantive results.[38] Similarly, the results of the LoI and the Farnborough Framework Agreement were limited. Indeed, the LoI led only to the creation of the Global Project Licences (GPLs), which proved to be of little use because the system was too complex – one defence-industry executive recalled that it took his company eight years to put together its first GPL request, due to disagreements between state parties.[39] It was this lack of progress in intergovernmental discussions that led the EC to step in.

The EC justified its intervention by pointing to the costs arising from the disjointed nature of the European defence market, and by arguing that if defence products could circulate more freely within the EU, it would help create a level playing field for European defence firms. The EC also took the view that facilitating intra-EU trade in defence products would improve the competitiveness of the European defence industry, while a more integrated European defence industry would serve the purpose of creating a common European defence and security policy.[40] The simplification of intra-EU controls was therefore presented as beneficial not only for the defence industry in economic terms but also for member states' military capabilities. The EC therefore pushed EU member states towards accepting an intra-community defence-trade directive by linking it with market-trade issues.

The EC's first step in trying to convince EU members was a 2003 communication entitled 'Towards a European Defence Equipment Policy',[41] in which it proposed the creation of common EU rules in the field of armaments production. This communication 'specifically addressed the need for simplifying intra-community transfers of defence-related products, whilst respecting Member States' prerogatives in this highly sensitive sector'.[42] Two years later the EC requested a 'fact-finding study', which was carried out by the consultancy firm UNISYS and published in February 2005 under the title 'Intra-Community Transfers of Defence Products'.[43] The study analysed the consequences of each country having its own rules for arms-export licensing and proposed steps towards harmonisation in order to make the internal market more efficient. It concluded that the multiple different licensing systems generated obstacles to intra-EU defence trade along with extra costs for companies when they applied for licences to export defence products to other EU states. This was the case despite the fact that almost all licence applications for intra-EU arms transfers were successful – in 2003, for example, only 15 applications were rejected while 12,627 licences were granted. The study concluded that obstacles to intra-EU defence trade were costing €3.16 billion (US$3.57bn) annually, and also noted that the LoI had so far produced meagre results. To tackle these issues, UNISYS proposed a new system that would include a number of different mechanisms: 1) a global licence for the whole of the EU; 2) a label for 'reliable' companies; 3) tracing of the movement of goods; 4) a one-stop shop for companies to obtain their export licences; and 5) a fallback option to allow states to deny an export licence if they saw the arms transfer as potentially posing a threat to their sovereignty (core interests). The idea at the time was that the EC and the European Defence Agency would be in charge of establishing the system.

Based on this assessment, the EC proposed the creation of a new instrument to facilitate the movement of defence products between member states, with countries' different licences for intra-EU exports replaced by a simplified common procedure. After a public consultation and workshops, a second study, 'Intra-Community Transfers of Defence Products – Impact Assessment', was published in December 2007.[44]

In December 2007 the EC presented a 'defence package' that included two directives, the first dealing with defence and security procurement, and the second – the ICT Directive – with intra-EU transfers of defence-related products.[45] The ICT Directive, applying to goods on the common EU military list, proposed three licences (general, global and individual) that would be common to all member states. It was therefore designed to facilitate the movement of military equipment between member states by harmonising arms-export authorisation processes for intra-EU transfers. The original UNISYS proposal that licences should be issued by EU institutions was abandoned, however: instead, member states would retain the power to issue licences for intra-EU exports.

EU member states were reluctant at first to accept the EC's proposal, partly because the six countries that had originally signed the LoI back in 1998 had little trust in the ability of the other member states to control their own arms exports.[46] It was certainly the case that the French were not particularly enthusiastic about the ICT Directive. Both the government and the defence industry initially opposed it, seeing it as unwelcome interference by the EC and an infringement on national sovereignty.[47]

This foot-dragging had already been seen in the French response to a European Commission consultation in 2006, following the UNISYS study, when the Secrétariat général des affaires européennes, a department attached to the prime minister's office, declared that it was 'premature to consider a [European Commission] initiative to apply the principles of internal markets and free movement to war materiel',[48] and also clearly expressed a preference for an intergovernmental approach via the LoI and COARM. The French government highlighted that the LoI had brought together the six countries with the greatest interest in defence-industry issues, and expressed the wish to continue discussing arms exports within that group.[49] In the opinion of of a civil servant in the Secrétariat général de la défense et de la sécurité nationale, the LoI at the time was still the most important forum for export-control discussions, and a more appropriate framework than that of the EU.[50] The French preference for intergovernmental cooperation, outside the EU framework, was voiced again in 2008 when senators expressed fears that the ICT Directive would lead to the decline of the LoI as a forum for discussions between major European arms manufacturers.[51]

Eventually, after years of negotiations, both the ICT Directive and the Common Position were agreed on at the end of 2008 – surprisingly during the French presidency of the Council of the EU, after France changed its negotiating stance. But, as will be explored in Chapter Four, while France was reconciling itself to these two initiatives at the European level, at the national level those who wanted to increase arms sales seized an opportunity to gain the upper hand and push aside those who preferred tighter controls. But first, Chapter Three will look at how France's arms-export policy underwent changes in the years immediately following the end of the Cold War.

OVERVIEW: A French arms-sales crisis, 1986–95

The total volume of French arms sales decreased significantly between the mid-1980s and mid-1990s. The period saw lower oil prices reduce the arms-purchasing ability of traditional customers in the Middle East, and also the end of procurement cycles in many other arms-importing countries. Moreover, with the end of the Cold War, not only did European markets contract but purchasing French arms no longer represented an attractive alternative to depending on either the United States or the Soviet Union. In this much more open and competitive environment, the previously strong position of French arms exporters was eroded. A further blow, after the Gulf War of 1990–91, was that Gulf states turned increasingly towards the United States for their arms purchases.

Major sales, 1986–95

Greece: 40 *Mirage* 2000 fighter/ground-attack (FGA) aircraft, ordered 1985, delivered 1988–92

India: 40 *Mirage* 2000 FGA aircraft, ord. 1982, del. 1985–86; 9 *Mirage* 2000 FGA aircraft, ord. 1986, del. 1987–88

Iraq: 300 AM-39 *Exocet* anti-ship missiles, ord. 1983, del. 1983–86; 19 *Mirage* F-1C FGA aircraft, ord. 1985, del. 1988–90

Saudi Arabia: 4 F-2000S frigates, ord. 1980, del. 1985–86; 24 *Shahine* surface-to-air missile systems, ord. 1984, del. 1986–90

Spain: 2 *Agosta*-class submarines, ord. 1977, del. 1985–86

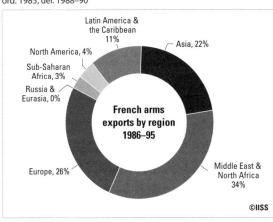

French arms exports by region 1986–95

Latin America & the Caribbean 11%
Asia, 22%
North America, 4%
Sub-Saharan Africa, 3%
Russia & Eurasia, 0%
Europe, 26%
Middle East & North Africa 34%

©IISS

Top ten customers, 1986–95:

1. Saudi Arabia
2. India
3. China
4. United Arab Emirates
5. Greece
6. Spain
7. Iraq
8. Egypt
9. United States
10. Finland

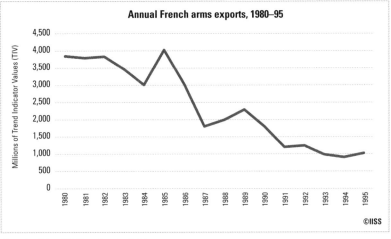

Annual French arms exports, 1980–95

Millions of Trend Indicator Values (TIV)

©IISS

Source for all data: SIPRI Arms Transfers Database

CHAPTER THREE

The ambiguity of French arms-export policy in the post-Cold War era

Following the end of the Cold War, the global arms market contracted and the French government's defence expenditure decreased significantly, causing the country's defence industry to incur major losses and shed jobs. The government's initial reaction was to seek to boost arms sales by streamlining the export-control process. Against the backdrop of a wave of privatisations, this was also a period that saw defence companies themselves doing more to promote their products overseas, with the government playing a lesser role. However, in the late 1990s a new government oversaw reforms within the defence bureaucracy that signified, if only for a few years, a somewhat greater commitment to exerting political control over France's arms exports.

Figure 3.1. **French arms-export policy after the end of the Cold War – chronology of reforms**

President	François Mitterrand (PS) 1981–95	Jacques Chirac (RPR/UMP) 1995–2007	Nicolas Sarkozy (RPR/UMP) 2007–12	François Hollande (PS) 2012–17	Emmanuel Macron (LREM) 2017–
Prime minister	Edith Cresson (PS) 1991–92; Pierre Bérégovoy (PS) 1992–93; Edouard Balladur (RPR) 1993–95	Alain Juppé (RPR) 1995–97; Lionel Jospin (PS) 1997–2002; Jean-Pierre Raffarin (UMP) 2002–05; Dominique de Villepin (UMP) 2005–07	François Fillon (UMP) 2007–12	Jean-Marc Ayrault (PS) 2012–14; Manuel Valls (PS) 2014–16; Bernard Cazeneuve (PS) 2017	Edouard Philippe (LR) 2017–
Defence minister	Jean-Pierre Chevènement (PS) 1988–91; Pierre Joxe (PS) 1991–92; François Léotard (UDF) 1993–95	Charles Millon (UDF) 1995–97; Alain Richard (PS) 1997–2002; Michèle Alliot-Marie (UMP) 2002–07	Hervé Morin (NC) 2007–10; Alain Juppé (UMP) 2010–11; Gérard Longuet (UMP) 2011–12	Jean-Yves Le Drian (PS) 2012–17	Sylvie Goulard (MoDem) 2017; Florence Parly (PS) 2017
International events that affected arms-export policies	1990–91: Gulf War; 1991: UNROCA; 1991: Luxembourg European Council criteria; 1996: Wassenaar Arrangement	1997: Ottawa Convention; 1998: Letter of Intent and Code of Conduct; 1999: OECD Anti-Bribery Convention (ratified by France in 2000); 2000: Farnborough Framework Agreement; 2001: 9/11 terrorist attacks	2008: global financial crisis; 2008: Oslo Convention; 2008: Common Position; 2009: ICT Directive	2013: start of war in Yemen; 2014: Arms Trade Treaty enters into force	
Domestic export-support reforms	1995: strategic plan for arms exports; 1990s: disappearance of the *Offices*	Oct 1999: 'coordinating committee' for arms exports at the Ministry of Defence; 1997: Europe removed from scope of DI; 2006: Fromion report	2007: stimulus package for arms exports; 2007: creation of CIEDES (renamed CIACI in 2008); Sept 2007: creation of 'war room' in Élysée; 2008: creation of PNSED and SOUTEX; 2011: defence attachés reform	2012–13: COMED replaces CIACI; end of war room; 2015: DAS replaced by DGRIS; 2015: Europe re-enters scope of DI	Belgium's purchase of armoured vehicles inaugurates new model for government-to-government contracting
Domestic export-control reforms	1990s: removal of first AP level (marketing)	2000: second AP level remains (negotiation and sale); 2000: export-control functions split between DI and DAS; 2004: Jean-Claude Mallet leaves SGDSN	2007: Jacques de Lajugie head of DI; 2008: DI regains export-control role; 2011: transposition of ICT Directive	2012–13: aborted export-control reforms • no reform on embargoes • no reform on dual-use export controls	

French arms exports — US$bn (current) — Orders / Deliveries

Year	Orders	Deliveries
1997	8.5	6.0
1998	7.8	
1999	9.6	5.7 / 4.7
2000	7.1	2.8
2001	3.9	3.1
2002	4.4	3.7
2003	5.1	5.2
2004	9.6	
2005	4.1	5.1
2006	7.2	5.1
2007	7.8	6.2
2008	9.7	4.7
2009	11.4	5.2
2010	6.8	5.0
2011	9.1	5.3
2012	6.2	4.3
2013	9.1	5.2
2014	10.9	5.4
2015		6.9
2016	15.4	7.9
2017	18.8	7.8 / 7.6

©IISS

Source: French parliamentary reports on arms exports, 2000–18

Political parties:
LR = Les Républicains; LREM = La République En Marche; MoDem = Mouvement Démocrate; NC = Nouveau Centre; PS = Parti socialiste; RPR = Rassemblement pour la République; UMP = Union pour un Mouvement Populaire; UDF = Union pour la démocratie française;
left-wing party   centrist party   right-wing party

1. 1990–2005: a period of wide-ranging changes

A new defence-industrial landscape

The end of the threat from the Eastern Bloc did not immediately cause France to reduce its defence expenditure. In 1989, when preparing a new five-year defence budget, the government had intended to maintain the level of spending, but 1991 proved to be a watershed year – the beginning of a downward trend in expenditure that would continue throughout the 1990s. With the exception of a brief slowdown in the mid-1980s, this was the first time since the mid-1950s that French defence spending had decreased in consecutive years (Figure 3.2).

As a consequence, the Ministry of Defence was unable to go ahead with all the armaments programmes that had been planned for the period 1990–95,[2] which was obviously a blow for the defence industry. This came at a time when foreign markets were also becoming more challenging for French arms companies. In fact, French arms exports fell by 66% between 1986 and 1995, a significantly greater contraction than that of the global arms trade over the same period (41%).[3]

The fall in export orders and the squeezing of the national defence budget precipitated a crisis for the French defence industry – in 1993, for example, it lost 10,000 jobs.[4] In 1991, two former directors of the Direction du développement international (DI) – a department in the Ministry of Defence that plays a major role in promoting arms exports (see Chapter One) – resigned from their positions: Hugues de L'Estoile, who was then working in Dassault's exports division; and Gérard Hibon, who was in Aérospatiale's international-affairs department. *Le Monde* journalist Jacques Isnard wrote that this double departure marked the end of an era characterised by arms sellers who had been, in Hibon's own words, 'shameless' in their approach to business,[5] and also that it signified

Figure 3.2. **French military expenditure, in US$m and as share of GDP, 1949–2000**[1]

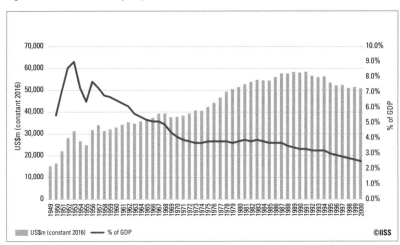

the end of the French arms trade's 'golden age'. That was an era when a large number of arms manufacturers were under direct state control, as too were many of the *Offices* that helped promote their products overseas, and when arms exporters had attracted customers with the argument that by buying French they could avoid dependence on either the US or the Soviet Union (see Chapter One). With the end of the Cold War, that sales pitch was no longer possible. Another event that contributed to French materiel losing some of its earlier appeal was the 1990–91 Gulf War, in which American weapons mostly proved superior to their French equivalents and, as a consequence, France's traditional customers in the Gulf turned increasingly to the US for their arms purchases.[6]

This was the context in which the French defence industry underwent a major restructuring. The wave of privatisations in the European defence industry reached France in the late 1980s, when a new right-wing government came to power, under prime minister Jacques Chirac, and privatised the missile and satellite manufacturer Matra in 1988, seven years after the Socialist government had nationalised it. In 1990, Lagardère, the owner of

Matra, forged an alliance with the GEC Group (UK) in the satellite sector. This established Matra Marconi Space as a joint venture between Matra Espace and Marconi Space Systems. In the helicopter sector, Aérospatiale's and Messerschmitt-Bölkow-Blohm (MBB)'s helicopter divisions merged in 1992 to create Eurocopter. Thomson-CSF acquired the defence-electronics activities of Philips in 1989. In 1996 the French–British joint venture Thomson Marconi Sonar was created, and Matra's tactical-missiles division merged with a division of the UK's BAE Systems, British Dynamics. In 1990 the French government modified the status of the land-armaments manufacturer GIAT, making it a state-controlled 'national company' and renaming it GIAT Industries. In October 1997 the government announced the privatisation of Thomson-CSF and Aérospatiale, although the state retained a 50% stake. This paved the way for further consolidations.

The electronics sector became centred around Thomson-CSF, which absorbed Dassault Électronique and the military activities of Alcatel Défense (communications systems). Thomson-CSF also took control of Sextant Avionique, a joint venture between Thomson-CSF and Aérospatiale. In the satellite field, a new company, Alcatel Space, was created from the satellite activities of Alcatel Défense, Aérospatiale and Thomson-CSF. The military-engine sector was rationalised in 2000 when the previously state-owned engine manufacturer Société nationale d'étude et de construction de moteurs d'aviation (Snecma) absorbed Turbomeca.

In the aerospace sector the first big change came with the privatisation of Aérospatiale and its merger with Matra Hautes Technologies to form Aérospatiale-Matra in July 1998. In 1999, 17% of Aérospatiale-Matra was floated on the stock market, the state retaining less than 50%. The government transferred its shares in Dassault Aviation to Aérospatiale-Matra, so the latter now owned 46% of the former. Aérospatiale-Matra produced military transport aircraft and, through its Franco-German subsidiary Eurocopter, military helicopters. In the space sector, the new company incorporated Aérospatiale's activities for strategic missile launchers and Matra's UK joint venture Matra Marconi Space, and was also involved in the tactical-missiles sector. The new group was short-lived, however, because in July 2000 it merged with Spain's CASA and Germany's DASA to form EADS. Also in 2000, Thomson-CSF acquired British company Racal Electronics and rebranded itself as Thales, thereby creating another European group. In 2001 the missile sector was restructured at the European level with the fusion of the missile activities of EADS, BAE Systems (UK) and Finmeccanica (Italy), creating MBDA.

A scandal and a change of government

French arms-export policymaking in the early 1990s was also affected by a major controversy surrounding earlier sales, and by shifts in the political landscape.

The controversy revolved around France's arms sales to Saddam Hussein's regime in Iraq during the previous decade. Between 1981 and 1990, France was the source of no less than 16.7% of Iraq's arms imports,[7] including military helicopters (the SA-342 *Gazelle*, SA-321H *Super Frelon* and SA-330 *Puma*); missiles (including HOT anti-tank, AM-30 *Exocet* anti-ship, and *Roland* surface-to-air missiles) and combat aircraft (*Mirage* F-1 fighters).[8] But in 1991, during the Gulf War, France provided the second-biggest European contingent (after the UK) in the coalition against Iraq – and when its forces found themselves facing an adversary armed with French weapons, a fierce debate ensued. The sight of French aircraft flying missions to destroy French military hardware was described in a *Le Monde* article as *l'arroseur arrosé* ('the sprayer sprayed').[9] Another aspect of the controversy was that France had exported technologies to a regime already known to have ambitions to build a nuclear arsenal and other weapons of mass destruction. Some parliamentarians reacted by demanding new regulations on arms exports. In November 1991, the UDF deputy Francois Léotard (later to become defence minister, 1993–95) suggested that a parliamentary committee should investigate French exports to countries violating human rights.[10] He also alleged that, during the Gulf War, 'some equipment of French origin … was found in larger quantities in our adversary's arsenal than in that of the whole French army'.[11] Meanwhile, François Fillon (later to become prime minister, 2007–12) proposed the creation of a permanent parliamentary committee to oversee arms exports.[12] Another proposal was for the regulation and oversight of the export-credit agency, the Compagnie française d'assurance pour le commerce extérieur (COFACE), with the deputy François d'Aubert arguing that the Gulf War had exposed the failings of France's export-insurance system.[13] None of these recommendations would be implemented, however.

As for the shifts in the political balance of power during the 1990s (see Figure 3.1), superficially there were few differences between the parties when it came to supporting arms exports. To take just a couple of examples: after PS defence minister Pierre Joxe tried to sell combat aircraft to Taiwan in 1992,[14] RPR prime minister Edouard Balladur made approaches to the Taiwanese regarding a potential sale of submarines in 1993;[15] and after UDF defence minister Charles Millon visited Saudi Arabia to promote the *Leclerc* main battle tank in 1995,[16] PS defence minister Alain Richard did exactly the same, on a number of occasions, from 1997 onwards.[17] However, one significant change, as described later in this chapter, is that the Socialist government that came to power in 1997 installed or promoted within the defence bureaucracy a number of political appointees and senior civil servants who advocated tighter controls on arms exports.

2. The state takes a step back

Adapting arms-export policy to a changed global market

In early 1997, before the election that gave the Socialists a majority in the National Assembly, President Chirac's defence minister Charles Millon presented a 'strategic plan' to boost arms exports.[18] With the slump in sales having already lasted ten years, the plan aimed to simplify export-control processes and better coordinate the government's export-promotion activities.

The plan was based on a 1996 report by Bruno Durieux, a former minister for foreign trade, which had been commissioned by prime minister Alain Juppé. In Durieux's opinion the low sales were not only due to the contraction of the world arms market but also showed that French defence products were becoming less competitive.[19] One of Durieux's major recommendations concerned export promotion. He wanted 'to anticipate, prepare and demand the necessary actions, and notably the contacts and interactions necessary in advance between political and operational decision-makers in the targeted countries and their French counterparts'. Durieux perceived deficiencies in the existing system, concluding that the Direction générale de l'armement (DGA) – and, within it, the DI – was not properly performing its coordination role. Another problem, in his view, was that the export brokers or *Offices* were becoming less relevant because all the defence manufacturers had by now created their own export structures. Durieux's report also concluded that the export-control process needed to be simplified; specifically it suggested removing the need for defence firms to obtain licences for market research and negotiations, pointing out that no other arms-exporting country had such a requirement.[20] In October 1996 Durieux was appointed as Millon's special representative for arms exports, responsible for strengthening France's relationships with potential customers.

The following year, Millon unveiled his strategic plan and the process of simplifying arms-export controls began. The plan was based on key aspects of the arms-export policy: 1) reorganising the geographical divisions of the DI around four main regions; 2) improving the coordination of export support through the creation of a new ministerial committee under the prime minister's leadership; 3) streamlining export-control processes; and 4) simplifying defence companies' access to export credit guarantees.[21] Millon left office following the 1997 elections that produced a Socialist-led coalition government, but some of the guidelines in the plan were implemented by the new administration. In October 1999, for example, a coordinating committee was created under the defence minister,[22] tasked with overseeing all major potential export deals and harmonising the ministry's high-level political and military contacts with arms-purchasing countries.[23] Millon's Socialist successor, Alain Richard, extended this initiative by introducing annual plans that set out the country's arms-export priorities.[24] There was also an increasing expectation that the French armed forces would become more closely involved in promoting arms exports.[25]

Alongside its goal of promoting exports, the strategic plan also aimed to streamline export controls. At the time, the main legislative texts framing the export-control procedure were decrees dating from 1939 and 1955 (No. 55-965). On the basis of these two texts, defence manufacturers who wanted to export their products had to obtain three *agréments préalables* (APs), granted by the Commission interministérielle pour l'étude des exportations de matériels de guerre (CIEEMG) – see Chapter One – and then, after signing a contract for a sale, an *autorisation d'exportation de matériel de guerre* (AEMG), which allowed the materiel to pass through customs. And even after the AEMG was granted, the company still needed to provide customs officials with yet another certificate, an *attestation de passage en douane* (APD).[26]

Civil servants in the DI had pushed unsuccessfully to remove one of the APs in 1991, during Edith Cresson's brief tenure as prime minister, and Millon made it clear with his strategic plan that he was determined to implement the streamlining process. He said his aim was to 'do away with unjustified complications in the licensing process, which has been found to be too slow and cumbersome'.[27] Eventually, by 2000, the number of APs was reduced to two, though the autorisation d'exportation de matériels de guerre (AEMG) and APD remained.

A greater export-promotion role for the defence companies

The French arms-export system was not immune to the neoliberal economic trends of the 1980s. In 1986, Jean-Pierre Bechter, a UMP deputy close to Serge Dassault, spoke in the National Assembly in favour of a more commercial approach:

> New private companies should be able to participate in seeking and signing new arms contracts, whether or not they use the official export brokers [i.e. the *Offices*]. Arms-export processes must enter the liberal era. The [market] environment is now so difficult that we can't just rely on state or state-related administrative structures.[28]

This exemplified an emerging market-oriented mindset that challenged the role of the state in arms exports and in the defence industry more generally. In 1988, Socialist defence minister Jean-Pierre Chevènement said he wanted to 'commercialise' the state's arms-export activities,[29] and a 1992 report published by the Fondation Saint-Simon, a think tank whose aims at the time included reconciling the Left to the market, argued that there should be more of a separation between the French state and the defence industry but also that state support should be made more effective.[30]

This marketisation process could be seen in the shifting roles of private and state actors. First, around the beginning of the 1990s, private defence companies formed associations as a means of mutual support in the face of the challenges posed by the post-Cold War defence market. The Comité Richelieu, created in 1989, aimed to improve access to the French armaments market for small and medium-sized companies; the Conseil des industries de défense (CIDEF) was founded in 1990 as an association to promote the interests of the defence industry; and the Groupement des industries de construction et activités navales (GICAN) was created shortly afterwards by companies in the naval sector. These organisations conveyed their members' demands for better export support from the government – for example in 1995 when the organisation representing the aerospace industry, GIFAS, complained of the government's 'modest' involvement in promoting arms exports and expressed its wish for assistance 'similar to that enjoyed by the US [defence] industry'.[31]

Defence companies also began creating new commercial and marketing departments, taking greater responsibility for promoting their products and thereby also performing the same role as the *Offices* (the partly or fully state-owned brokers for arms sales – see Chapter One) and, to a certain extent, the DI. In 1988, Dassault Aviation created an international-trade department, primarily as a response to customers' increasing demands for offsets.[32] In 1989, Aérospatiale launched its export subsidiary, aiming to better adapt offset packages to clients' needs.[33] Also in 1989, Thomson-CSF created a trading company to assist with offset packages for a *Mirage* 2000 deal in Greece.[34] In 1991, Aérospatiale and its German partner founded a company to promote Eurocopter products.[35] The same year, state-owned DCN created a private company, DCN-International (DCN-I), to facilitate access to international markets.[36] In 2000, Thomson-CSF became Thales. Two years later, Thales and DCN created a joint marketing company, Armaris, which took over DCN-I's activities.

These changes had significant implications for the *Offices*, as they were now just one among a number of vehicles for promoting French defence equipment overseas. They became increasingly marginalised during the 1990s as newly privatised defence companies began using their own sales departments to engage directly with customers.[37]

The role of the *Offices* was also challenged politically. In 1989, in the wake of a report by the Ministry of the Economy that criticised their public status and also their opaque operations,[38] a privatisation process began. In 1999 the *Offices* were negatively impacted by the entry into force of the OECD Anti-Bribery Convention, because their role had always included dispensing commissions to local intermediaries.[39] Indeed, in the case of arms deals on behalf of the state-owned manufacturers, the *Offices* had handled bribes so as to ensure the state was not directly involved.[40] The French state officially relinquished control over many of these export brokers through a decree published on 15 June 2000,[41] a step that some media commentators said was taken for the specific purpose of conforming with the new anti-bribery convention.[42] By 2018, the only *Office* still partly under state control was Défense Conseil International (DCI), which provides training services in support of French arms-export contracts.

But according to the economically liberal mindset of the time, disappointing arms sales could be partially explained by excessive state involvement. It was thought that if the state took a step back and created space for private actors to play a greater role, French companies would have a better chance of winning export contracts.[43]

At the same time, state entities working on export promotion were weakened. In the 1990s the DGA was also exposed to the unfavourable headwinds for civil servants involved in supporting arms exports. Indeed, against the backdrop of the post-Cold War transformations and the slump in French arms sales, the DGA was made something of a scapegoat for the defence industry's problems. It was widely perceived as being too bureaucratic to adapt to changed circumstances, and as an obstacle to the necessary reforms. The DGA and its armaments engineers were also criticised for being too focused on technological aspects of armaments programmes rather than keeping costs in check and attending to the actual needs of the armed forces.[44] Its fiercest critics were within the Ministry of Defence itself: the chiefs of staff; the administrative department, the Secrétariat general pour l'administration (SGA); and the newly created political department, the Délégation aux affaires stratégiques (DAS).[45] As a result the DGA underwent a series of reforms in 1986, 1994 and 1997, aimed at reducing costs. In the opinion of a former Ministry of Defence official, the introduction of new public-administration methods at the DGA was significant because it represented a 'retrenchment of the state', with the defence firms themselves now expected to do more to promote sales.[46]

There were also warning signs for the DI – the export-promotion department within the DGA – about a possible reduction in its role. In 1986, defence minister André Giraud had instructed the DI to let defence firms take greater responsibility for commercial negotiations,[47] and in 1987 he commissioned a report which concluded that 'exports must be the prime responsibility of the industries, as the state must not interfere with their job … the state's intervention will be now limited to endorsement, not the political side of sales.'[48] In 1988, an idea emerged for a 'super federator' for arms exports, acting at a level above the DI.[49] Another omen was the appointment in 1990 of a defence-industry executive, rather than an armaments engineer, as DI director.[50] A few years later, the DI would be stripped of some of its responsibilities.

On 17 January 1997, all 'armaments cooperation' issues were transferred from the DI to the Direction de la coopération et des affaires industrielles, another department of the DGA,[51] which meant that the DI's export-promotion role no longer included helping to sell French arms to other European countries.[52]

3. A short-lived parenthesis

A more restrained approach to arms sales after 1997

The narrowing of the DI's role continued after the change of government in 1997 when a Socialist prime minister, Lionel Jospin, was elected. Since the 1960s the DI had been responsible for both export promotion and export control, but in August 2000 it was stripped of the latter role when the handling of defence companies' applications for export licences was transferred to the DAS,[53] the Ministry of Defence's political department. This was not just a deliberate weakening of the DI but also a shift towards a more cautious control process under the Socialist government. Within the defence bureaucracy the roles of arms-export promotion and control would be split between the DI and DAS for eight years, until 2008.

The new government also took steps to strengthen France's arms-export controls at the international level by committing to a number of agreements. It ratified the Ottawa Convention on anti-personnel mines in 1997; the European Code of Conduct (see Chapter Two) in 1998; and the OECD Convention on Combating Bribery of Foreign Public Officials in International Business Transactions (or OECD Anti-Bribery Convention), which obliged firms to comply with transparency norms when signing international contracts and prohibited the payment of commissions to local intermediaries or politicians, in 2000.[54]

It was mainly the continuing reverberations of scandals such as the Taiwan frigates affair that had pushed France to ratify the Anti-Bribery Convention, and doing so inevitably implied a loss of competitiveness in the international arms trade, in particular with customers such as Saudi Arabia. Indeed, in a report presented in the National Assembly,[55] the convention was viewed as potentially having a very serious impact on arms sales. Voices in the French media, meanwhile, exclaimed that 'nothing will be as before'.[56] But in the words of a former Ministry of Defence official, with the ratification of the Anti-Bribery Convention the French arms-export system 'moved from an ancient form of trade to the modern world'.[57] Under French law, penalties for non-compliance with the convention included hefty fines and even prison sentences, and the risk of sanctions changed the way that French defence firms dealt with intermediaries in other countries. As the journalist Alexandra Schwartzbrod colourfully put it in a *Libération* article in 1999, there would be 'no more fruit salesmen recruited in this or that country to pass on suitcases full of banknotes'.[58] The new regulation replaced the existing French system of *frais commerciaux exterieurs* (FCEs) or external commercial fees. Previously, French defence firms had simply reported FCEs – the costs of commissions paid to intermediaries – to the Ministry of the Economy and were subsequently reimbursed through deductions from their corporation tax.[59]

The move towards tighter controls
The more cautious approach to arms exports came just a couple

of years after Millon had set out his plan to boost arms exports by streamlining the export-control process. Under the new Socialist government that came to power in 1997, there was a group of actors – the leaders of the DAS and the Secrétariat général pour la défense et la sécurité nationale (the defence and foreign-policy office of the prime minister – see Chapter One), and the political staff in the office of the defence minister, Alain Richard – who favoured tighter export controls. They believed the DI was vulnerable to conflicts of interest because it was responsible for both export promotion and export control, and that those two roles needed to be carried out by separate entities within the Ministry of Defence bureaucracy. For evidence of laxity in the control process, they could of course point to the long list of French arms-sales controversies over the years and find cases when the drive to increase arms exports seemed to have led to injudicious sales.

At the upper levels of the arms-export bureaucracy, the new Socialist government appointed civil servants who favoured a more restrained approach. According to a former defence minister, the government did not dissent from the traditional doctrine of providing state backing for defence exports, but it was anxious to avoid repeats of earlier controversies.[60]

Within the Ministry of Defence, the department that would acquire greater importance – and resources – at the expense of the DI was the DAS, the political department of the Ministry of Defence, whose work included defence diplomacy and analysis of geopolitical trends. It had been created in 1991 as a direct auxiliary of the office of the defence minister, and therefore its position in the bureaucracy was close to those who wielded political power, offering the prospect that it would be able to subject arms-export decisions to greater political scrutiny.[61] Its first director was Jean-Claude Mallet, who stayed in the position until 1998 and became one of the key actors pushing for the institutional separation of export-support and export-control activities within the Ministry of Defence – or, more specifically, the transfer of the export-control role from the DI to the DAS.

Other significant officials involved in the reform were Christian Lechervy, who was international-affairs adviser to Socialist defence minister Alain Richard between 1997 and 2002, and had previously worked in the DAS and also for a non-governmental organisation; and Jean-Bernard Ouvrieu, appointed as Richard's special representative for arms exports in October 1998. Lechervy was in favour of the reform, but Ouvrieu, although tasked with implementing it, was less enthusiastic.

At Richard's request, Ouvrieu submitted a reform proposal in a report in June 1999, which was important in preparing the ground for the reform. Ouvrieu's words during a Senate hearing in December 1999 also provide a neat summary of the thinking of those behind the reform: 'The preparation of export decisions submitted to the CIEEMG will from now on be given, with the DGA's technical support, to the DAS, in order to better take into account the political dimension of exports.'[62]

The institutional resources of those in favour of tightening controls were reinforced in the monthly CIEEMG meeting (see Chapter One). Until 1987 the CIEEMG had been attended only by civil servants, but episodes such as the Luchaire affair precipitated a long process of making the CIEEMG more 'serious', in the words of a senior civil servant, by including political staff from the ministers' *cabinets* and also, as observers, members of the intelligence services.[63] This increased the number of voices arguing for a more cautious approach to arms sales – and, again, more specifically, for the separation of the export-support and export-control roles.

But the DI did not give up its export-control responsibilities without a fight. In response to the proponents of the reform, who argued that the decision-making process within the

Ministry of Defence was skewed in favour of promoting arms exports, DI director Philippe Roger insisted that the checks and balances between export promotion and control were securely in place in the next stage of the process, the CIEEMG, in the form of discussions between senior representatives of the Ministry of Defence, the Quai d'Orsay and Bercy.[64] The DAS, for its part, was set on becoming the primary bureaucratic interlocutor for the defence industry and taking from the DI the role of vetting and filtering defence companies' applications for export licences before passing them on to the other Ministry of Defence departments and other ministries.[65]

The reform, implemented through decree No. 2000-807 on 25 August 2000, was described by defence minister Alain Richard as 'an improvement in the implementation of controls',[66] while a former DI official saw it as 'a way to limit [arms] exports to a necessary evil'.[67] Forty civil servants were transferred from the DI to the DAS, with the latter now becoming the place where French defence firms presented their export-licence applications. Ahead of the monthly interministerial CIEEMG meeting, the DAS also took responsibility for synthesising its own stance with the opinions of the DGA and the Defence Staff during the *pré-CIEEMG* held with the defence minister's political advisers.[68] This also meant the DAS was in charge of presenting the unified Ministry of Defence position to the representatives of the other ministries during the CIEEMG. The coalition of actors who advocated a more cautious approach to arms sales had made an advance, at least temporarily.

There was no significant change in the pattern of France's arms sales, however. In the early years of the twenty-first century, French defence companies continued to export to their traditional customers, particularly in the Middle East. It was evident, therefore, that a more rigorous bureaucratic process did not automatically change final outcomes.

France's ambiguous stance on the EU Code of Conduct

Despite the changes that took place under the Jospin govern-ment (1997–2002), France's lack of enthusiasm towards the British proposal for a European Code of Conduct on arms exports was a further indication that those who favoured a more cautious approach to arms sales were not completely dominant. Launched in the summer of 1997, the proposal came from Tony Blair's newly elected Labour government and was partly the result of pressure from British NGOs. The new British foreign secretary, Robin Cook, was eager to begin discussions on the Code of Conduct with the newly elected Socialist government in France, aiming to secure a bilateral agreement that could then be submitted to the other EU member states.[69] The French govern-ment expressed support, with Jospin welcoming the prospect of a 'code of good conduct prohibiting the sale of armaments for internal repression or external aggression',[70] but behind the scenes the negotiations were far from straightforward.

The UK held the presidency of the Council of the EU in the first half of 1998, and used its position to promote discus-sion on arms-export controls at the European level. A first Franco-British draft of a Code of Conduct was sent to all EU member states on 23 January 1998, but the French reservations that emerged during the subsequent negotiations were the main reason why it proved impossible to reach an agreement within the EU working group on arms control, COARM.[71] Several drafts were discussed during the following months, and it became clear that French officials did not want the Code of Conduct to be very restrictive.[72] A final text was agreed in May, but because of French objections it had to be weaker than the British had originally envisaged.[73] For example, France rejected proposals regarding public and intergovernmental transparency,[74] and objected to tighter versions of the criteria on human rights and development.[75]

In fact, from the French perspective, the main purpose of the Code of Conduct was not to prevent arms sales to regimes that violated human rights but instead to prevent unfair competition between Europe's arms-exporting states, which explains why the denial-notification mechanisms were included in the code. Also, France preferred to discuss arms exports primarily with the British, rather than with other European states, because only the UK had a defence-industrial base, and export-control processes, comparable to its own.[76] For the French it was useful, therefore, to join the British initiative as a way of keeping a close eye on the drafting of the Code of Conduct and exerting as much influence as possible. In that respect it was also convenient, of course, that the British were seeking French support. These factors why, despite its underlying reticence towards the idea of a Code of Conduct, France nonetheless went along with the process initiated by the UK.

OVERVIEW: A period of transition, 1996–2005

From the early 2000s onwards the arms trade was fuelled by renewed modernisation programmes in Europe, Asian economic growth and increasing oil revenues in the Gulf countries. French firms benefited from this return to growth, with Dassault Aviation, Thales (then Thomson-CSF) and Naval Group (then DCNS) securing key contracts that eased the transition to the post-Cold War environment. Overall, the French defence industry did not significantly diversify its client base after the end of the Cold War; there was a large degree of continuity in the geographical distribution of its arms exports. Shifts in the balance of political power in this period did not appear to impact directly on sales: export-promotion attempts during the years of the Socialist government showed that internal bureaucratic reforms did not automatically produce different outcomes.

Major sales, 1996–2005

Brazil: 1 *Clemenceau*-class aircraft carrier, ordered 2000, delivered 2001 (second-hand)

Chile: 1 *Scorpène*-class submarine, ord. 1997, del. 2005

India: 6 *Scorpène*-class submarines, ord. 2005, del. 2017; 10 *Mirage* 2000 fighter/ground-attack (FGA) aircraft, ord. 2000, del. 2004–05

Pakistan: 2 *Agosta*-90B submarines, ord. 1994, del. 1999–2003

Qatar: 12 *Mirage* 2000-5 FGA aircraft, ord. 1994, del. 1997–99

Saudi Arabia: 3 F-3000S frigates, ord. 1994, del. 2002–04

Taiwan: 6 *La Fayette*-class frigates, ord. 1991, del. 1996–98; 60 *Mirage* 2000-5 FGA aircraft, ord. 1992, del. 1997–98

United Arab Emirates: 390 *Leclerc* tanks, ord. 1993, del. 1994–2006; 62 *Mirage* 2000-5 Mk-2 FGA aircraft, ord. 1998, del. 2003–07

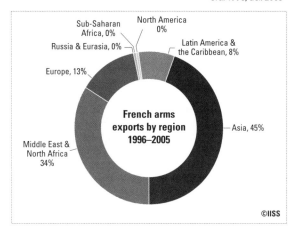

French arms exports by region 1996–2005

- Sub-Saharan Africa, 0%
- North America 0%
- Russia & Eurasia, 0%
- Latin America & the Caribbean, 8%
- Europe, 13%
- Asia, 45%
- Middle East & North Africa 34%

©IISS

Top ten customers, 1996–2005:

1. Taiwan
2. United Arab Emirates
3. China
4. Saudi Arabia
5. Pakistan
6. Turkey
7. Brazil
8. South Korea
9. Qatar
10. Chile

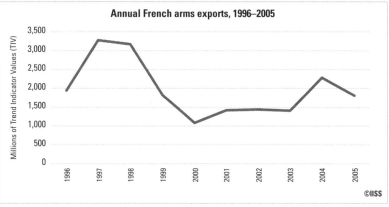

Annual French arms exports, 1996–2005

©IISS

Source for all data: SIPRI Arms Transfers Database

CHAPTER FOUR

President Sarkozy's stimulus package for arms exports

French arms-export policy changed course again in the early years of the twenty-first century, as a perceived decrease in demand for French defence manufacturers' products provoked calls for more state support, which in turn led to the implementation of a new reform agenda. At the same time, the international negotiations that would culminate in the 2014 Arms Trade Treaty (ATT) paradoxically weakened French civil-society organisations that were advocating tighter domestic controls on arms exports, while the balance of power within the French arms-export bureaucracy tilted back towards those who favoured a more liberal approach. European discussions also had an impact on the French arms-export-control process, as those who wanted to boost arms sales were able to use a European directive to their advantage.

1. Towards a renewed agenda for arms-export support

Scandals without repercussions

In the 2000s there were arms-export scandals that seemed to have potential repercussions for policymaking but ultimately had little impact because of the weakness of French anti-arms-trade non-governmental organisations (NGOs). 'Angolagate', concerning illegal arms sales to Angola that had taken place in the mid-1990s during the country's civil war, led to prominent French politicians and businessmen being taken to court, including former interior minister Charles Pasqua. There was also a sale of submarines to Malaysia, which would eventually become linked to murder investigations and allegations of kickbacks reminiscent of the infamous Taiwan frigates affair; and the *affaire Karachi*, when the deaths of 15 people, including 11 French naval engineers, in a terrorist bomb attack in 2002 were allegedly connected to the cessation of a series of illicit payments following a sale of submarines to Pakistan in 1994.[1] In both cases the French media again focused narrowly on the theme of corruption, without questioning the country's broader arms-export policy.

This was a period when French anti-arms-trade NGOs were concentrating on international advocacy campaigns rather than domestic policy. When Amnesty International and Oxfam launched the ATT campaign in October 2003, their French affiliates also became involved. But while they were backing the ATT and also the EU Common Position (see Chapter Two), the French NGOs' limited resources meant they could not simultaneously address arms-export policy at the national level. They also lost an ally in 2004 when Jean-Claude Mallet, a proponent of a more rigorous export-control process (see Chapter Three), stepped down as head of the Secrétariat général de la défense et la sécurité nationale (SGDSN), though he later returned to defence policymaking during the preparations for the Defence and Security White Paper in 2008.[2]

Defence-industrial actors in search of state support

By the mid-2000s the French government and defence-industry leaders had begun to worry about a lack of international

Figure 4.1. **French arms exports – orders and deliveries (in US$bn), 1997–2006[3]**

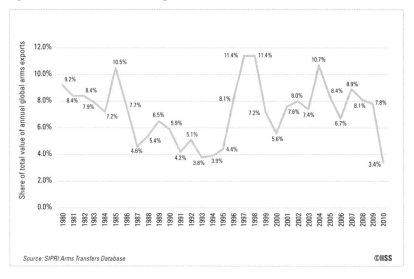

Source: French Ministry of Defence – various reports to parliament on French arms exports   ©IISS

Figure 4.2. **France's share of the global arms trade, 1980–2010[5]**

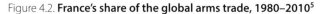

Source: SIPRI Arms Transfers Database   ©IISS

demand for French defence products. A decline in foreign orders was a major cause for concern, obviously implying a future decrease in production. As Figure 4.1 shows, the total value of arms deliveries actually rose between 2000 and 2004 but the total value of orders decreased.

This fuelled a perception that French armaments were becoming less competitive and the country's arms-marketing campaigns less successful. In 2007, French officials estimated that the country had been overtaken by Russia as the world's third-biggest arms exporter, which was seen as a serious failure.[4]

A sense of urgency began to spread among arms-export policymakers, and the government announced its aim to increase exports to a value similar to that of domestic arms procurement – €8–10 billion (US$12–15bn) per year.[6] There was a belated realisation that the global arms market had changed, and a reassessment, for example, of the previous assumption that France could count on achieving 10–15% of total global sales of combat aircraft. According to a former political appointee in the defence minister's *cabinet*, it was this realisation that led eventually to a reorganisation of the French arms-export system.[7] The Ministry of Defence and also the defence companies themselves came to believe that the increasing complexity of arms-deals negotiations required government and industry to adopt a more coordinated approach.

Although there is data to suggest that French arms exporters were actually faring better in the mid-2000s than during most of the 1990s (see Figure 4.2), the *perceived* slump in sales was the main argument for a more vigorous approach to promoting arms exports, and for increased state support in particular. In 2004, the association representing the defence industry, the Conseil des industries de défense (CIDEF), argued that the global defence economy was slowing and international competition intensifying, and therefore that the French government should improve export-support coordination and revise export-control procedures.[8] Three years later, in its 2007 white paper, the CIDEF demanded a renewed dialogue between government and industry so as to make arms exports 'a national priority'.[9]

Defence manufacturers also began to protest against the reform that had split the roles of export promotion and control between the Direction du développement international (DI) and the Délégation aux affaires stratégiques (DAS) in 2000 (see Chapter Three). The new division of responsibilities reduced the level of interaction between the staff in the two departments. Moreover, many now regarded the export-control process as increasingly cumbersome – for example, a Direction générale de l'armement (DGA) official who had previously worked in a defence company commented that there had been 'a dispro-portionate development of control' since the 2000 reform,[10] while according to a right-of-centre politician 'the CIEEMG [Commission interministérielle pour l'étude des exportations de matériel de guerre] … had become suffocating'.[11] It was indeed the case that companies' applications for export licences could become lost in the bureaucratic maze, and the CIEEMG could take up to six months to decide whether to grant a licence.[12] Some defence-industry executives complained that the DAS seemed obstructive towards to any arms sale, even when the buyer was as uncontroversial as Greece or Spain.[13]

A DGA official recalled that as the defence companies became increasingly concerned about bureaucratic obstacles, they began to appeal to the defence minister through the CIDEF.[14] In the words of a member of the new team of senior civil servants that took over at the DI in 2007, 'when we asked the companies how to improve state support, they answered that we shouldn't complicate things for them, but instead should simplify [export] controls'.[15] This sentiment would lead to a reversal of the 2000 reform.

A new agenda with powerful backers
In January 2006, concerned by the perceived lack of foreign orders for French materiel, defence minister Michèle Alliot-

Marie suggested that a UMP deputy in the National Assembly, Yves Fromion, should write a parliamentary report on how state support for arms exports could be improved.[16]

The Fromion report would have a significant impact on policymaking, with its key proposals inspiring a number of reforms. Fromion called for a new commission to coordinate export support, which was duly created in 2007 in the form of the Comité interministériel pour les exportations de défense et de sécurité (CIEDES), and recommended that it should draw up a 'national strategic plan' for arms exports. He suggested that the activities of one of the *Offices*, the Société française d'exportation de systèmes d'armement (SOFRESA), should be expanded beyond Saudi Arabia. He also proposed that the armed forces' significant involvement in promoting sales of French materiel abroad should be recognised, formalised and also properly funded by the government.

On the export-control side, Fromion's main proposal was to replace the *agrément préalable* (AP) procedure with a *déclaration d'intention d'exporter*, a process in which a defence company could assume its application for an export licence had been granted unless the CIEEMG issued a negative response within 30 days. He also advocated the extension of the global licences, and echoed the calls for better communication between government and industry.[17]

The Fromion report made policymakers pay closer attention to the issue of arms-export support, and was one of the factors that contributed to the appointment of Jacques de Lajugie as director of the DI in December 2006. De Lajugie came from the Ministry of the Economy, where he had been director of the department for foreign trade and had overseen, during a posting to Dubai, French trade with the Middle East – a commercial relationship in which arms sales were a major component. Another of his previous roles was as financial director for the Ministry of Defence.[18] He therefore boasted a strong background both in trade and defence, a likely asset when it came to interministerial coordination. A former DGA official also pointed out that in the eyes of the defence minister, Michèle Alliot-Marie, the fact that de Lajugie came from the Ministry of the Economy made him more likely to offer reliable, objective advice rather than represent the interests of the armaments-engineer corps.[19]

After his appointment, de Lajugie quickly gained a seat at the monthly CIEEMG meetings alongside the representatives from the DAS and the defence minister's *cabinet*, becoming the first DI director to participate in the meetings since the 2000 reform.[20] This represented a significant return to power for the DI within the export-control process.

But despite the publication of the Fromion report and de Lajugie's appointment, it was only after Nicolas Sarkozy took office as president, in May 2007, that the next reforms to French arms-export policy took place.

2. From the *Rafale* to reforms

The failed *Rafale* campaign in Morocco
In addition to the Fromion report, a failed sales campaign in Morocco was another factor increasing the pressure for changes to the arms-export-support apparatus. In 2005–06, King Mohammed VI indicated to President Jacques Chirac that Morocco had an interest in buying French combat aircraft. Dassault Aviation subsequently offered Morocco 18 *Rafale*s for €1.8bn (US$2.3bn), but the issue of how to finance the deal soon became problematic because the country was already heavily in debt to France. The Ministry of the Economy hesitated for months over granting Morocco a loan, and then Chirac himself refused to decide because his term of office was due to end in a

matter of weeks. In the early spring of 2007, as the negotiations dragged on, it emerged that the American company Lockheed Martin was offering Morocco its F-16 as an alternative. The delays continued after Sarkozy's election as president in May 2007. In June the prime minister's office suggested that 12 *Rafales* could be sold instead of 18, but the Moroccans rejected the idea. When Paris finally agreed in July to provide credit to fund the purchase of all 18 aircraft, it was too late: Morocco had already decided to buy 24 second-hand F-16s instead.

The failure to sell the *Rafales* to Morocco was widely regarded as indicating a lack of coordination between the different parts of the arms-export apparatus, and was a key trigger for the reforms that would be implemented in the autumn and winter of 2007.[21] After Sarkozy came to power in May 2007, the new government took the view that there were failures of communication – for example between the DGA and the defence industry, on pricing – and too many divisions within the industry itself.[22]

The Moroccan fiasco was in fact the latest in a succession of failures to sell the *Rafale*, for example in South Korea in 2002, Singapore in 2005 and Saudi Arabia in 2006. Combined with the fact that foreign orders for French arms in the period 2001–06 were still below the level of the late 1990s, this fuelled the perception that urgent action needed to be taken.

A new president: Nicolas Sarkozy's approach to arms sales
Nicolas Sarkozy's frenetic governance style and his close advisers' personal connections with the DI leadership were key factors in shaping arms-export policymaking during his 2007–12 term of office. He depicted his election victory as marking a clear change – *la rupture*, as he put it – and presented himself as being much more proactive and reform-minded than his predecessor Chirac, despite being from the same party (UMP).[23]

Sarkozy actually intensified the centralisation of power, steering a number of policy areas directly from the Élysée.[24]

Under Sarkozy, the highest levels of the French state became actively involved in seeking to boost arms exports. A Quai d'Orsay official recalled that during Sarkozy's time in office there was particular pressure exerted on those in charge of arms-export controls to process defence companies' export-licence applications more quickly.[25] It was not only the DGA/DI that was expected to help boost the arms-sales figures: France's ambassadors abroad were also instructed to exert themselves in support of the country's defence industry.

The impetus to boost arms exports was increased by the personal connections between staff in the president's office and DI director Jacques de Lajugie – indeed, in the 2007–11 period the DI had direct contact with the Élysée, circumventing the Ministry of Defence's normal processes.[26] For example, de Lajugie had a line of communication to Claude Guéant,[27] who was general secretary at the Élysée during the early part of Sarkozy's presidency and therefore one of the president's closest aides.

In the words of a former DGA civil servant:

> De Lajugie would, for example, on [an arms sale to] Libya, call Boris Boillon, who worked for Claude Guéant on this topic. If there was a question, a problem, we knew that Boillon's answer had the blessing of Guéant and sometimes of Sarkozy himself. There were meetings on Saturday mornings to decide on certain cases.[28]

De Lajugie therefore had a significant degree of influence, which increased the political clout of the DI and other actors in favour of boosting arms sales during this period, and ultimately played an important role in the changes that were to come.

3. Export support: state actors return to the fore

With Sarkozy in the Élysée and de Lajugie at the head of the DI, many proposals from the 2006 Fromion report were implemented. A stimulus package (*plan de relance*) was adopted in the second half of 2007, containing a number of reforms aimed at improving arms-export promotion and streamlining control procedures.

In September 2007, a so-called 'war room' for military and civil exports was set up at the Élysée, aiming to win major contracts by taking a leading role in sensitive negotiations that required direct engagement between heads of state.[29] At different times, two of Sarkozy's closest collaborators ran the war room: Edouard Guillaud, the presidential chief of staff, until February 2010, and then Guéant until February 2011.[30]

In August 2007 the government made another statement of intent when prime minister François Fillon announced at the annual conference of French ambassadors the imminent creation of the CIEDES. The CIEDES began operations in October, and in 2008, after also taking on responsibility for non-military exports, became the Commission interministérielle d'appui aux contrats internationaux (CIACI). The CIACI's objective was to organise the state's logistical support for arms exports: unlocking credits for guarantees, coordinating France's ambassadors in their contributions to arms-export-promotion efforts, and pushing arms sales onto the agenda during presidential or ministerial visits abroad.[31] The CIACI's meetings aimed to define the precise roles of the various participants in an arms-sales campaign, so as to make the bureaucratic process faster and more efficient.[32]

Another coordination instrument created as part of the stimulus package was the *Plan national stratégique des exportations de défense* (PNSED). These plans, the first of which was drafted in the summer of 2007, provided an overview of potential defence exports, specifying products, potential buyers and the actions that needed to be taken to maximise the chances of achieving sales.[33]

The government also wanted to strengthen the military's involvement in export promotion, and its first step was to reform the network of defence attachés working at French embassies around the world. Previously there had been two categories of attachés – 'defence attachés', who were military personnel and reported to the Defence Staff (EMA), and 'armaments attachés', who were armaments engineers and reported to the DGA – but between 2008 and 2011 they were merged.[34] The new attachés were all expected to become involved in promoting sales of materiel, a task previously devolved to the armaments attachés.[35] A further indication of the intention behind the reform was that future defence attachés would now receive a week of training at the DGA, including information on governmental arms-export support and three days of meetings with defence companies.[36]

The 2007 stimulus package also created a small export-support unit (Soutien aux exportations – SOUTEX) within the EMA, consisting of three military officers.[37] Its purpose was to harmonise and better monitor the export-promotion efforts of the three armed forces; all promotion activities, and their costs, now had to be reported.[38] The creation of SOUTEX was partly a response to the French defence industry's growing requests for assistance from military personnel (in order to demonstrate the use of equipment, for example), which placed added strain on the armed forces' resources.[39]

Another reform concerned one of the remaining *Offices* or export brokers, SOFRESA (see p. 27), which became ODAS in April 2008. The state bought 34% of the shares in the new entity (it had held only 5% of SOFRESA), which was tasked with covering the Middle East as a whole, whereas SOFRESA had focused only on Saudi Arabia.[40] This was interpreted as a move by the government to achieve greater control over arms-export negotiations in this key region for French defence firms.[41] Ten years later, in 2018, ODAS was closed down in response to a request from the Saudi Arabian government.[42] All of these developments represented something of a comeback for state actors in the domain of arms-export support, following the period of retrenchment described in Chapter Three.

4. Export control: the convergence of national and European interests

The stimulus package launched in the second half of 2007 also contained measures aimed at facilitating the administrative procedure through which defence companies obtained export licences. Two major reforms in particular were implemented during President Sarkozy's term of office (2007–12): the return of the export-control role from the DAS to the DI, in 2008; and the transposition, in 2011, of the EU Intra-Community Transfers Directive in order to simplify the control procedures both for intra- and extra-EU arms exports.

The DI regains its powerful position

In 2008, the transfer of export-control responsibilities from the DI to the DAS, which had taken place in 2000 (see Chapter Three), was reversed. With this important change, the DI was again tasked with both export promotion and export control, while the DAS was reduced to playing a coordinating role for the Ministry of Defence at the CIEEMG meetings.[43] The reform was clearly aimed at streamlining export-control processes and therefore boosting arms sales. The 2006 Fromion report had recommended, for example, that export-control processes should be adapted to 'ambitions in terms of exports',[44] while the defence minister from 2007 to 2010, Hervé Morin, spoke of 'smoothening' and 'modernising' control processes as a means to increase sales.[45]

The government's priorities were also reflected by a change to the wording of part of the government's annual finance bill. In 2008, export controls came under the heading of 'defence diplomacy', as a contributor to 'conflict avoidance',[46] but in 2009 they were moved into the 'export support' category, reflecting the fact that the export-control process was now seen as subservient to export promotion.[47]

And although proponents of a more restrained approach to arms sales back in 2000 had criticised the DI for being too close to the defence industry, using that as a justification for taking away its responsibility for assessing companies' licence applications, by 2008 the ability to communicate fluidly with the defence industry was seen in a much more positive light. According to Morin, the objective of the reform was 'to better take into account the needs of our companies, who ask us to quickly answer their questions'.[48]

This new narrative logically meant that responsibility for overseeing the export-licensing process would return to the DI. However, this change did not take place without an internal struggle within the bureaucracy. The package of export-support reforms proposed by the Ministry of Defence in 2007 reportedly even considered placing the DI under the responsibility of the DAS.[49] The battle between the two departments then spilled into the public arena. In December 2007, during a public hearing in the National Assembly, DAS director Jean de Ponton d'Amécourt issued a warning to those who wanted to reverse the 2000 reform, insisting that it had been 'wise'.[50] His successor Michel Miraillet also publicly resisted the reorganisation of export controls, arguing that the DI's responsibilities should not extend beyond export promotion. He said that 'serious controls' were needed in response to the defence industry's somewhat indiscriminate approach to finding customers.[51] The reorganisation of export controls within the Ministry of Defence was debated again during the preparation of the 2008 Defence and National Security White Paper, which happened to be coordinated by Jean-Claude Mallet, a proponent of the 2000 reform.[52] The decision to return the export-control role to the DI was taken after heated discussions between Mallet and de Lajugie.[53]

When it was published in June 2008, the white paper stated that France's arms-export policy rested on three principles, the first being 'to ensure, within the state, and at all levels – interministerial and ministerial – the separation of the control and support functions, which guarantees the absence of conflicts of interests'.[54] It initially appeared, therefore, that the DAS had succeeded in resisting the change. However, a month later it was reported that the government had decided to return to the DI '60 of its civil servants involved in looking into sales issues',[55] which confirmed that the DI had won the battle and that the 2000 reform had effectively been reversed.

The transposition of the ICT Directive: using Europe for a national reform

Until 2014, despite attempts to streamline the arms-export-control process, it remained complicated. Originally, as described in Chapter Three, there were three *agrément préalables* (APs) – for market research, negotiations and contract signature – along with an *autorisation d'exportation de matériels de guerre* (AEMG) and, finally, an *attestation de passage en douane* (APD). Simplification, to a degree, began with the removal of the AP for market research in 2000, followed by the substitution, from 2006, of 'global AEMGs' for batches of single AEMGs,[56] and in 2007 the merging of the APs for negotiations and contract signature into a single AP.[57]

The Sarkozy government was determined to expedite the licensing system for arms exports, for example adopting the goal of processing half of all export-licence applications electronically by mid-2008. Next, the adoption of the EU Common Military List in 2009 simplified the categories of defence equipment subject to export controls, although France did add two categories of its own to the EU list – satellites and space-launch vehicles.[58]

But the most significant change by far came with Law No. 2011-702 of 22 June 2011, after the French parliament voted for a more radical reform based on the European Commission's ICT Directive. The transposition of the ICT into French law would entail the simplification of export controls for arms transfers to other EU countries, but French legislators also decided to extend it to extra-EU arms exports.

The ICT Directive delineated three types of 'transfer licence' – general, global and individual – that would supersede France's previous layers of controls (AP, AEMG, APD), eventually enabling defence companies to negotiate, sign a contract and export their products in a single step. With the removal of the AP and AEMG, which became effective in 2014, the French arms-export-control system reversed its defining principle, in place since 1939: *ex ante* controls (*contrôle a priori*) gave way to *ex post* controls (*contrôle a posteriori*).[59]

The change was expected to reduce the average time taken to process a defence company's export-licence application from 110 days to 50, and to cut by more than half the total number of administrative decisions that needed to be taken in the CIEEMG process, from 14,000 per year to 6,000.[60] The CIEEMG meetings could now focus solely on the most important or sensitive export-licence applications. The DI, meanwhile, took advantage of the reform to overhaul its IT system, aiming to fully computerise the export-licence-application process.

As explained in Chapter Two, French defence policymakers had not initially been enthusiastic about the idea of the ICT Directive, put forward by the European Commission in 2007 – but by the end of 2008 there would be a volte-face, with the ICT Directive agreed at the EU level during the French presidency of the Council of the EU (hereafter referred to as the 'EU presidency').

In the SGDSN in particular – but also among civil servants in the Ministry of Foreign Affairs and the Ministry of Defence, and in the defence industry itself – there was apprehension at the prospect of EU institutions interfering in French arms-export policymaking. According to a DGA official, the perceived risk was that the ICT Directive could open the way to the French government's decisions on arms exports being challenged in the European courts.[61]

Because the SGDSN was in charge of harmonising arms-export controls with five other European countries within the intergovernmental Letter of Intent (LoI) framework (see Chapter Two), it would rather have maintained that approach than adopt an EU-wide instrument such as the ICT Directive. However, since its creation a decade earlier, the LoI had not achieved very much in terms of harmonising European export-control procedures. The European Commission's ICT proposal, which was significantly more ambitious than the LoI in terms of harmonising arms-export controls, was in fact presented just as the LoI, after about eight years of work, was preparing to implement new joint-licensing procedures.[62] A civil servant in the Ministry of Defence's legal-services department explained that there was a degree of rivalry between the French officials working on the LoI and European bureaucrats who favoured the ICT Directive.[63]

The LoI's lack of results was precisely one of the arguments used in favour of the ICT Directive by those in the French government who wanted to streamline the arms-export-control process. This could be seen in the words of a 2008 report, also authored by Yves Fromion: 'it was largely the assessment that the LoI had made very limited progress in this area that led the [EC] to put forward [the ICT Directive]'.[64]

As for what eventually persuaded France to accept the ICT Directive during its EU presidency in the second half of 2008, the explanation lies in a power struggle within the government bureaucracy, won by those who wanted to increase arms sales by simplifying export controls. These individuals made use not only of the French government's desire to demonstrate progress on European defence cooperation during the country's EU presidency,[65] but also the lobbying of the French government by the EC. The instructions from the Élysée and the Ministry of Defence to France's representatives at the EU in Brussels were that a final draft of the ICT Directive had to be agreed upon before the end of the country's presidency.[66]

French eagerness gave the EC some leverage. A DGA official described how the EC convinced the Ministry of Foreign Affairs, which wanted to achieve political gains during the French EU presidency, that its defence package was the perfect medium for that purpose.[67] Another Ministry of Defence official provided a similar account of the EC strategically presenting the defence package as a reform that had already been prepared for implementation during the presidency – and on a subject France itself wanted the EU to make progress on.[68]

Those who favoured simpler arms-export controls also saw the ICT Directive as an opportunity to simplify not only intra-EU but also extra-EU arms-export controls. A DGA official, for example, explained that he and many of his colleagues recognised that the transposition of the directive could be a convenient vehicle for a more far-reaching streamlining process.[69] One of those colleagues, recalling conversations with those who opposed the reform, said the following:

> People didn't want to reform the system. The sticks-in-the-mud saw the ICT as a threat. But I told them – it's coming anyway, and if we don't adapt our system now, the arms-export system will be completely blocked. … We used the ICT to convince them to reform.[70]

His point, essentially, was that if the ICT Directive was transposed into French law and yet France's regulations for extra-EU arms exports remained as before, the country would find itself burdened with two parallel export-licensing processes.

Pressure on government was also exerted through a third Fromion report, published in 2010. According to a DAS official, those in favour of extending the ICT Directive's simplified control process to extra-EU arms exports anticipated that the publication of the formal report could help their cause and break the stalemate between the DI, which was backing the reform, the SGDSN, which opposed it, and the Ministry of Foreign Affairs, which was hesitating on the issue.[71]

There was also an intricate legal argument employed to convince the prime minister, the defence minister and their respective *cabinets* to accept the ICT Directive – and it was linked to the ongoing debates regarding the upgrading of the EU Code of Conduct on arms exports to a legally binding Common Position (see Chapter Two).[72] France had made its acceptance of the Common Position conditional upon the lifting of the arms embargo against China (see Chapter Two), and was seeking to convince the US, which was vehemently in favour of maintaining the embargo, that the Code of Conduct was already sufficient to prevent such a rise in arms transfers to Beijing.[73] In 2008, however, France performed a volte-face on the Common Position, accepting it without the China embargo having been lifted. There were two main explanations for this change of position: externally, the China embargo was becoming less of an issue among European countries,[74] and internally, a significant legal link was forged between adhering to the Common Position and accepting the EC's proposal for the ICT Directive.

In the six months before France took over the EU presidency in July 2008, according to a civil servant working in the Ministry of Defence's legal department at the time, the looming prospect of the ICT Directive set off a major legal dispute among French officials. For some, it gave rise to fears that the EC could eventually exert influence over EU member states' arms-export policies.[75] The jurisprudence was from Case 22/70 (31 March 1971) in the European Court of Justice, known as the ERTA (European Agreement on Road Transport) judgment, which ruled, in summary, that the EC could gain sole external jurisdiction over a field in which it had developed intra-EU regulations. Or in this case, in the words of the same Ministry of Defence official, the EC could potentially move on from harmonising rules for intra-EU defence sales to ruling on EU members' arms exports to the rest of the world.[76]

The French government looked for a legal strategy that would prevent the EC from extending its competences to extra-EU arms exports. It seemed – to summarise the legal narrative – that accepting the Common Position might ensure that decisions regarding extra-EU arms exports would remain in the intergovernmental domain and not fall into the EC's jurisdiction further down the line. That, essentially, is why France changed its stance on the Common Position.[77] And with the Common Position seemingly providing a potential shield against what the French government saw as EC overreach, it was more amenable to the prospect of the ICT Directive.

The adoption of the ICT Directive in 2009, and its transposition into French law in 2011, streamlined licensing procedures for arms sales to customers both inside and outside the EU. This was a victory, clearly, for those who wanted a more dynamic approach to arms exports over those who favoured greater caution.

The Arab Spring: a missed opportunity to strengthen export controls

In the first half of 2011, debates in the French parliament on the transposition of the ICT Directive took place against the backdrop of the Arab Spring and claims by international NGOs that, in many of the countries where uprisings were taking place, Western-supplied equipment was being used by the security forces against demonstrators. A few months later, Amnesty International produced a list of Western arms sales to Bahrain, Egypt, Libya, Syria and Yemen since 2005.[78] Although in some countries the outcry led to the adoption of more restrictive arms-export policies,[79] this was not the case in France.

Aiming to influence the debates in the National Assembly and the Senate on the law transposing the ICT Directive, French NGOs drew a connection between Western arms sales and the suppression of protests in Arab countries. The French affiliates of Amnesty International and Oxfam, and CCFD-Terre Solidaire, argued that the imminent transposition of the ICT Directive into French law should be used as an opportunity not to liberalise but to strengthen the French arms-export-control system.[80]

After the start of the revolution in Tunisia in December 2010, the issue of French arms exports to the country aroused intense media interest, although that was due less to NGO campaigning than to a statement in parliament by the foreign minister, Michèle Alliot-Marie. On 11 January 2011, Alliot-Marie announced in the National Assembly that France was considering providing the Tunisian government with equipment and training for its security forces.[81] The announcement provoked a hostile reaction from opposition politicians and the media. It was later discovered by the media that the government had agreed a sale of riot-control equipment to Tunisia in late 2010 but then – belatedly – blocked delivery.[82] The eruption of the civil war in Libya in February 2011, meanwhile, also led NGOs and the media to question France's recent arms sales to the Gadhafi regime.[83]

In parliament, however, only Europe Écologie Les Verts (EELV)[84] and the Parti communiste français (PCF)[85] used the Arab Spring as an argument to tighten French arms-export controls, which they thought might be possible through the inclusion of European export-control criteria in French law, and therefore tabled amendments to the bill transposing the ICT Directive. Conversely, the two big parties, the UMP and the Socialists, welcomed the streamlining of arms-export-control processes through the ICT Directive, and almost none of their deputies or senators made reference to the Arab Spring protests as a factor that might have a bearing on French arms-export policy.[86] The exception was a UMP senator, Josselin de Rohan, who felt obliged to insist that despite the simplification of arms-export controls, France would still be able to cancel any licences authorised for sales of defence equipment to controversial customers.[87] The amendments put forward by the EELV and the PCF were not adopted. The law transposing the ICT Directive, and therefore simplifying France's arms-export-control process, was passed on 22 June 2011, when state repression in the context of the Arab Spring was still ongoing.

OVERVIEW: French arms sales back on track, 2006–17

In this period French arms exporters continued to focus on customers in the Middle East and North Africa – including some controversial ones. In 2007–08, for example, contracts were signed with the Gadhafi regime in Libya for the modernisation of *Mirage* F-1 combat aircraft and the sale of *Milan* anti-tank missiles; negotiations also began for the sale of 14 *Rafale* combat aircraft, but stopped at the outbreak of the country's civil war in 2011. Between 2008 and 2011, there were unsuccessful attempts to sell a border-defence system worth US$1.5–2 billion to Saudi Arabia, and *Rafales* to the United Arab Emirates. In the second half of the 2010s, French arms exporters benefited from a favourable international context and also from French military operations in sub-Saharan Africa and the Middle East, which served to showcase the country's military equipment. Orders for *Rafales* were received from Egypt and Qatar in 2015, and from India in 2016.

Major sales, 2006–17

Australia: 12 *Attack*-class submarines, ordered 2016, planned delivery 2033–50

Brazil: 4 *Scorpène*-class submarines, ord. 2009, del. planned 2020–25; 1 nuclear-powered attack submarine, ord. 2009, del. planned 2029

Egypt: 4 *Gowind*-2500 frigates, ord. 2014, del. 2017; 1 FREMM frigate, ord. 2015, del. 2015; 24 *Rafale* fighter/ground-attack (FGA) aircraft, ord. 2015, del. 2015–18; 2 *Mistral* amphibious assault ships, ord. 2015, del. 2016

India: 6 *Scorpène*-class submarines, ord. 2005, planned del. 2017–21/22; 49 *Mirage* 2000-5 FGA aircraft, ord. 2011, planned del. 2015–23; 36 *Rafale* FGA aircraft, ord. 2017, planned del. 2019–22

Malaysia: 6 *Gowind*-2500 frigates, ord. 2014, planned del. from 2019; 1 *Scorpène* submarine, ord. 2002, del. 2009

Qatar: 24 *Rafale* FGA aircraft, ord. 2015, planned del. 2018–20

Singapore: 6 *La Fayette* frigates, ord. 2000, del. 2007–09

South Korea: 214 EC155 helicopters, ord. 2015, planned del. 2022; 66 *Crotale* NG surface-to-air missile systems, ord. 2003, del. 2006–09

United Arab Emirates: 62 *Mirage* 2000-5 Mk-2 FGA aircraft, ord. 1998, del. 2003–07; 17 *Ground Master*-200 air search radars, ord. 2013, del. 2015–17; 2 *Helios*-2 reconnaissance satellites, ord. 2015, del. ongoing

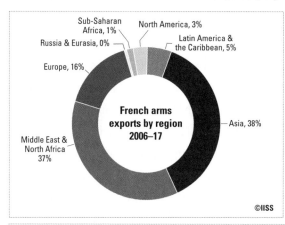

French arms exports by region 2006–17

- Sub-Saharan Africa, 1%
- North America, 3%
- Russia & Eurasia, 0%
- Latin America & the Caribbean, 5%
- Europe, 16%
- Asia, 38%
- Middle East & North Africa 37%

©IISS

Top ten customers, 2006–17:

1. Egypt
2. United Arab Emirates
3. Singapore
4. China
5. Morocco
6. Greece
7. India
8. Saudi Arabia
9. Australia
10. South Korea

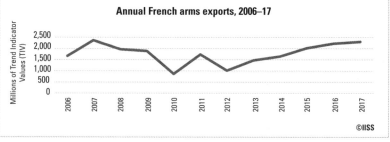

Annual French arms exports, 2006–17

Millions of Trend Indicator Values (TIV)

©IISS

Source for all data: SIPRI Arms Transfers Database

CHAPTER FIVE

President Hollande: continued backing for arms sales

1. The perceived need for increased arms sales at times of economic crisis

Economic considerations influenced French arms-export policy during François Hollande's five years as president (2012–17). The defence industry suffered as a result of cuts to the defence budget made at the start of Hollande's term of office, although defence spending later rebounded in response to the Islamist terrorist attacks that took place in 2015. The five-year *Loi de programmation militaire* (LPM) that set out the defence budget for 2014–19 was quite restrictive, with little room for manoeuvre after Hollande's campaign promises to reduce the public deficit. Also, the 2014–19 LPM assumed that a substantial number of combat aircraft would be exported during that period. It planned for the air force to receive 26 *Rafale*s over the five years, but the manufacturer, Dassault Aviation, needed to produce 11 *Rafale*s per year, and therefore 66 over the five-year period, to keep the production line open – a production rate guaranteed by a contract with the state.[1] This meant that at least 40 *Rafale*s needed to be exported – otherwise, because the state guaranteed the production of 11 *Rafale*s per year, it would have to buy them itself, from the air force's budget. But the LPM did not set aside any funds for this possible additional procurement of 40 combat aircraft.[2] This is a good indication of how arms exports are a crucial factor in the French state's military budgeting: any shortfall in exports would end up being paid by the taxpayer.

In addition to budget constraints, the Hollande government also faced an unemployment crisis. The defence industry did not hesitate to play the jobs card when it requested increased state support,[3] as it did in a July 2012 white paper from the Conseil des industries de défense (CIDEF).[4] The CIDEF chairman also emphasised that exports were 'an indispensable industrial complement in terms of workload' and that without them the industry simply 'couldn't manage'.[5]

At the time, calls for export support went far beyond the defence domain. The new foreign minister, Laurent Fabius, was relaunching the concept of 'economic diplomacy', which essentially meant placing renewed emphasis on the ways in which foreign policy could be used to serve France's economic interests. As part of this initiative, in April 2014 the Ministry of Foreign Affairs took over the running of trade departments that had previously been part of the Ministry of the Economy – the first time during the Fifth Republic that the Quai d'Orsay had taken bureaucratic responsibility for foreign trade – and created a new directorate for enterprises and the international economy.[6] These administrative changes gave a boost to arms-export support, as indicated for example in the yearly report to parliament on arms exports.[7] Fabius strongly believed that the Quai d'Orsay needed to contribute to the country's economic recovery, and the consequences of this new dynamic within the ministry included an increase in the number of civil servants tasked with promoting defence sales.[8]

2. Policy reforms: revising the role of state actors

In the Ministry of Defence, arms-export support was also reorganised under the new minister, Jean-Yves Le Drian, a long-time political associate of President Hollande. Export controls, meanwhile, underwent very little change during the 2012–17 Socialist government.

Reforming arms-export promotion: a change of instruments

With regard to arms exports, Le Drian set out to rebalance the roles of the ministry and the defence industry. His idea was that the ministry should take the lead in initiating political and strategic discussions with potential customers, and that only afterwards should the firms offer their specific products. In October 2012, following a visit to the United Arab Emirates, Le Drian indicated that he did not bring up the *Rafale* combat aircraft during the trip because in his view it was up to the defence industry to make commercial offers.[9] Or in other words, the role of the defence minister was to create the appropriate political conditions in which the French defence industry could subsequently secure arms deals.[10] This approach was formally stated in the annual report to parliament on arms exports, and a new coordinating body, the Comité des exportations de défense (COMED), was created within the Ministry of Defence to help implement it. The locus of decision-making on arms exports therefore returned to the Ministry of Defence from the Élysée, where the 'war room' and the Commission interministérelle d'appui aux contrats internationaux (CIACI) created under Nicolas Sarkozy were abandoned.[11]

The COMED's role included assisting the defence minister in examining issues and documents related to arms exports, and facilitating coordination and communication on international contracts. Importantly, the Direction du développement international (DI) served as the secretariat for the COMED, which meant deciding on its agenda and writing up the minutes of the meetings.[12] These new structures were intended to address perceived failures during the previous years. Between 2007 and 2012, arms-export promotion had been centralised in the Élysée, where negotiating methods were regarded by some as brusque. The war room, led by Claude Guéant, had been the cornerstone of the system, but centralisation did not always mean effectiveness. In the view of a former Direction générale de l'armement (DGA) official, centralisation at the Élysée created a dysfunction because it interfered with the work done at the prime ministerial level. While the CIACI embodied an intra-governmental approach, bringing together various departments, its work was circumvented by ad hoc, informal meetings at the Élysée organised by Guéant.[13] The existence of two decision-making centres created coordination problems[14] – precisely what the COMED was created to address. A defence-industry executive complained that, in 2007–12:

> Industry representatives were not part of the CIACI. The war room effectively made the CIACI redundant. There were actually two levels – the war room, where the industry participated, and the level of the departments. But what was required was overall coordination and a flow of information between the senior decision-makers, the bureaucracy and the firms. It was a time of top-down control by Nicolas Sarkozy.[15]

A former DGA official was also harsh in his view of the CIACI, explaining that it became inefficient since it met only every two months and included too many people, none of whom had any decision-making power.[16]

An additional problem with export promotion under Sarkozy had been the negotiating style. The political leadership had a tendency to publicly discuss the progress of arms-deal negotiations,[17] which not everyone considered helpful. A former DGA official, for example, commented that most customers would rather not have their defence procurements discussed in the media.[18] Another ex-DGA civil servant, while acknowledging the active involvement of the political leadership at the time, also recognised that such an attitude could be 'irritating' for their counterparts in arms-purchasing countries.[19] The clearest example of this had been in 2009, when Sarkozy and his team prematurely announced that they had secured a contract to sell 36 *Rafale* combat aircraft to Brazil,[20] but in fact Brazil eventually decided to buy Swedish *Gripens* instead.[21] In the view of a DGA official, 'in Brazil, we missed it because Sarkozy announced that we sold it … just before the [Brazilian] elections'.[22] Also, the arms-export-support system between 2007 and 2012 had lacked effective prioritisation, despite the creation of the *Plan national stratégique des exportations de défense* (PNSED) in 2008. Although the PNSED had categorised deals as either 'priority' or 'non-priority', what happened in practice was that all export campaigns eventually ended up under the 'priority' label.[23]

As well as the rebalancing of the roles of government and industry under President Hollande and his defence minister Jean-Yves Le Drian, the period 2012–17 also saw state actors become even more proactive in supporting arms exports. Firstly, an in-depth institutional reform occurred in the Ministry of Defence, with the Délégation aux affaires stratégiques (DAS) transformed into the Direction générale des relations internationales et de la stratégie (DGRIS) in 2015.[24] The DGRIS was bigger than its predecessor, and its status as a 'general directorate' meant that its director occupied one of the most senior positions in the Ministry of Defence.[25] The change had an impact on arms-export policymaking as the DGRIS took charge of managing the international network of defence attachés, whose principal responsibilities included promoting French arms abroad.

The creation of the DGRIS was first mooted in the spring of 2012. The move was seen as a means to diminish the power of the chief of the Defence Staff, which had increased since 2005,[26] and to rationalise the internal workings of the Ministry of Defence, where there were numerous overlapping roles and diluted responsibilities.[27] The reform, formally announced on 31 July 2013, was justified on the grounds that the way the ministry conducted its international relations was inefficient, and that the work involved needed to be concentrated in a single department.[28] Le Drian specified in a speech in 2014 that export-promotion work would remain the remit of the DI and not be affected.[29]

The creation of the DGRIS was part of a broader reform of the defence ministry, and did not directly concern arms exports. However, because the DGRIS became responsible for the defence attachés, the move did have an impact on various stakeholders in arms-export policy. Significantly, whereas the DAS had generally pursued a more restrained approach to arms sales, the DGRIS was more geared towards supporting arms exports.

In addition, the DI was strengthened. It regained the European geographical zone in terms of export support, which had been given in the 1990s to another DGA department, the Direction de la stratégie (DS) (see Chapter Three). According to the legislative texts governing the organisation of the DGA, Western Europe was within the DI's purview from January 2015,[30] while an organisational decree for the DGA abrogated the articles containing the DS's responsibility for armaments cooperation in Europe.[31] The scope of the DI's responsibilities was therefore broadened.

Another state actor involved in arms-export support received similar reinforcement – Défense Conseil International (DCI), the last of the export brokers or *Offices* left over from the Cold War era. In December 2013, Jean-Michel Palagos, deputy director of Le Drian's office, became DCI's CEO, and under his leadership its activities were expanded. DCI signed an agreement with Nexter, broadened its activities to aerial-surveillance services and partnered with SOFEMA to create a new company for the maintenance of *Alouette* helicopters worldwide. Through these initiatives DCI developed as a provider of services for the French armed forces, which had not been its original purpose,[32] and at the same time it refocused on arms-export support and training services for buyers of French weapons, and also began to expand beyond the Middle East to develop other markets.[33]

Export controls: the status quo prevails

In comparison with the changes made to the arms-export-support apparatus, export controls were somewhat neglected between 2012 and 2017. Indeed, it was an area in which the government abandoned two reforms.

When the Socialists came to power in May 2012, anti-arms-trade non-governmental organisations (NGOs) had high expectations due to Hollande's earlier statements. During the election campaign he indicated that he wanted 'a strong, coherent and controlled defence industry', including increased transparency in general and new controls on brokering activities.[34] As president, his first address to the UN General Assembly also implied a change in approach.[35] For the first two years of the new government, in a gesture towards greater transparency, defence minister Le Drian went in person to the National Assembly and Senate to present the annual report on arms sales, but on each occasion his audience was conspicuously small and, due to this evident lack of interest, the initiative was abandoned after 2013.

NGOs were particularly disappointed by the failure to enact a reform regarding arms-embargo violations and arms-export brokering that the Hollande government had indicated it would pursue.[36] The draft bill on the violations of arms embargoes was originally approved by the government in 2005 – but it was only in 2007 that the Senate adopted a first version of the bill. Under Hollande, the National Assembly's foreign-affairs and defence committees did not receive the draft bill for discussion until January 2016.[37] Parliamentarians and NGOs in favour of the reform accused the government of stalling the legislation because it would have complicated arms transfers to rebel groups in the ongoing conflicts in Libya and Syria.[38] As of December 2019, the legislation remains in draft form, as its second reading by the Senate has still not been scheduled.[39]

Another reform promise concerned the export-control system for dual-use products (i.e. those with military and civilian applications). Unlike the export-control process for military materiel – administered mainly by the Ministry of Defence and the Secrétariat général de la défense et la sécurité nationale (SGDSN), via the Commission interministérielle pour l'étude des exportations de matériels de guerre (CIEEMG), as described in Chapter One – the process for dual-use goods is handled by the Service des biens à double usage (SBDU), which is part of the Ministry for the Economy, and the Commission interministérielle des biens à double usage (CIBDU), chaired by the Ministry of Foreign Affairs.[40] Before he was elected, Hollande indicated his intention to merge the processes by 'assembling under the same authority our control instruments for dual, civil and military, defence and security technologies, which are too scattered'.[41] This proposal was then taken up in the 2013 Defence White Paper, which indicated that it was important to bring closer together the export-control instruments for civil and military technologies designed for defence and security use, in order to improve the overall efficiency of the export-control system.[42] A commission was set up to provide recommendations on how to proceed, based on the premise that the separation of the export-control processes for military materiel and dual-use goods led to inefficiency and incoherence. The circulation of information was impeded by a lack of communication between the two processes and the fact that the two export-control commissions, CIEEMG and CIBDU, had different IT systems. The results of the report were presented to the prime minister, Jean-Marc Ayrault, in December 2013.[43]

The report's main proposal was to create a new interministerial authority that would supervise the export processes for both military materiel and dual-use products. The authority would not replace the existing systems and bureaucracies but would oversee their activities. Its responsibilities would include allocating cases to either the CIEEMG or the CIBDU, ensuring better cooperation between departments, and deciding on the most sensitive cases or passing them on to higher levels in the government. The authority would in effect represent an initial step towards a planned merger of the CIEEMG and CIBDU. It would also coordinate with the Ministry of Foreign Affairs on external diplomatic activities related to export controls; define a communication strategy towards the industry; coordinate communications across ministries and the development of common IT systems; and determine the CIEEMG's and CIBDU's internal rules.[44]

However, none of these proposals were ever implemented. The report was quickly buried and the idea of merging the export-control processes for military materiel and dual-use products was never mentioned again publicly. This raises the question of why the idea was put on the presidential agenda in the first place, going all the way to François Hollande's 2012 presidential campaign. Originally the idea of merging the two export-control processes came from the same actors who had initiated the 2000 reform splitting export support from control within the Ministry of Defence (see Chapter Three). According to a ministry official, it was Christian Lechervy – who had been involved in the 2000 reform, having already been in favour of a more restrained approach towards arms exports at that time – who included the idea in a campaign speech for Hollande in March 2012.[45] This created a strong political case for including the reform in the new white paper.

A key motive for the reform stemmed from the discrepancies between the CIEEMG and the CIBDU, and the lack of interaction between the two systems. The same Ministry of Defence official explained that the individuals who favoured the reform originally wanted the SGDSN to take charge of export controls for both military materiel and dual-use-goods.[46] They also took the view that the CIBDU did not have robust processes, as it had no internal regulations and therefore lacked a process for interministerial coordination. A similar issue was that there were no high-level guidelines for the export-control process for dual-use goods.

However, the status quo prevailed due to resistance from actors in the government and the defence industry who wanted to increase arms sales. The industry expressed opposition to the possibility of dual-use goods becoming subject to the stricter export-control rules for military equipment via a CIEEMG-type procedure,[47] fearing that the controls would be too cumbersome as a result.[48] A Quai d'Orsay official who favoured the status quo said it was problematic to send the wrong signals to the industry.[49] As for the Ministry of the Economy, which was at the heart of the export-control process for dual-use goods, it opposed the change because it would lose a degree of control over the process if it came to be seen from a defence angle rather than an economic one.[50]

3. The boom in French arms exports after 2012

Numerous major arms-export contracts were signed during President Hollande's term of office between 2012 and 2017. Orders for French materiel were soaring, and indeed reached an all-time record of €16.9 billion (US$18.8bn) in 2015.

The twists and turns of the *Mistral* deal

Before it achieved a string of successes on the arms-sales front, the Hollande administration had to handle a delicate situation that it inherited from the Sarkozy government – that of the sale of two *Mistral* landing-helicopter-dock amphibious assault ships (LHDs) to Russia. The deal, signed in June 2011, originated from a Russian request first expressed to the French government at the Bourget naval show in October 2008, two months after the war in Georgia.[51] At the time, the decision to sell the *Mistral*s to Russia had been made on the basis of economic and diplomatic considerations.

On the diplomatic front, French officials had envisaged that the deal 'could represent an important step in the "normalisation" of trade relations between Paris and Moscow',[52] and the negotiations had taken place between 2008 and 2011 in the context of a general rapprochement between Russia and the West.[53] In the Élysée the perception was that 'the Cold War was over' and that Russia should be dealt with as a partner, not a rival.[54]

As for the economic factors, they concerned the companies involved in manufacturing the *Mistral*s: DCNS (which became Naval Group in 2017), the state-owned shipbuilding company, responsible for designing the vessels; and partly state-owned STX, which built their hulls. STX, a vital economic presence in the Atlantic port of Saint-Nazaire, was in difficulty and shedding jobs. It primarily built cruise ships but that market had shrunk considerably after the 2008 global financial crisis. The government made STX a symbol of the fight against unemployment, and in September 2008 President Sarkozy himself visited its shipyard, pledging to act personally to obtain contracts.[55] In this context the *Mistral* deal was extremely important, and although the construction of the two ships would take up only 20% of the shipyard's capacity, it would maintain 1,200 jobs for four years.[56]

The *Mistral* deal also had symbolic value. At the time, Sarkozy and his government were pushing hard to obtain foreign orders for the *Rafale* combat aircraft, but without success. In the absence of *Rafale* sales, it was politically valuable for the government to be able to announce that it had secured a significant armaments contract with Russia.

However, as soon as France and Russia started negotiating the sale of the *Mistral* warships, protests were voiced by French allies. Firstly, six United States senators wrote a letter to the French embassy regarding the projected transfer.[57] In early 2010, US secretary of defense Robert Gates visited France and, in bilateral meetings with defence minister Hervé Morin and President Sarkozy, also conveyed the US concerns.[58] One of Gates's key arguments was that the *Mistral* sale would send the 'wrong signal' to Russia and also to Eastern European states.[59] In other meetings, US representatives voiced worries about technology transfers.[60] Eastern European countries were also worried about the deal: the Baltic states, Poland, Ukraine, Romania and Georgia protested against it in numerous different arenas and tried to exert diplomatic pressure on Paris via the US administration,[61] NATO and the EU.[62]

Ultimately, however, economic considerations were more important and the deal was signed in 2011. In the words of one of the US diplomatic cables that surfaced through WikiLeaks, 'The French, like the Americans, they said, seek to sell weapons in order to help their economy and to create employment.'[63]

Less than three years later, renewed competition between Russia and the West triggered protests that unseated Ukraine's president, after which Russia seized Crimea and funded an anti-government insurrection in the Donbas region. Meanwhile, the first amphibious assault ship, the *Vladivostok*, began sea trials in March 2014, and was scheduled for delivery in October 2014. The second *Mistral* ship, the *Sebastopol*, was scheduled for delivery in 2015.

When the protests began at the end of 2013, the French reaction was initially to assert that the unfolding events in Ukraine did not affect the military cooperation between France and Russia. When the *Vladivostok* began its trials, the Élysée repeated the message. In mid-March 2014, foreign minister Laurent Fabius indicated that France would reconsider the deal only if other European countries took action against Moscow – for example, he said, if the UK were to freeze Russian oligarchs' financial assets in London.[64] France maintained this stance between March and September 2014, indicating that the *Vladivostok* would be delivered as planned in October. In June, 400 Russian sailors travelled to Saint-Nazaire to train on the ship. In July the EU introduced additional economic sanctions against Russia following the downing of flight MH17. These included an arms embargo, although it did not apply to contracts signed prior to 1 August 2014[65] and therefore allowed the French government to continue asserting that the delivery of the *Vladivostok* would proceed. But then, on 3 September 2014, Hollande announced that 'the conditions that will allow France to authorise the delivery of the first [amphibious assault ship] have so far not been met'.[66] This decision to place the delivery on hold came just before the NATO Summit in Wales on 4–5 September, and at a time when Russia's counter-offensive was achieving military gains in eastern Ukraine.

This French announcement was a subtle way to respond to international pressure while still leaving the door open to the deal if the situation in Ukraine evolved in a more peaceful direction. The Russian sailors continued to train in France, and Russia continued to make the agreed payments. In November 2014, however, Russia indicated that it would shortly issue a formal demand for financial compensation.[67] In the meantime, on 22 November, the second *Mistral*, the *Sebastopol*, put to sea in Saint-Nazaire, which obviously indicated that the building of the warships had not been interrupted despite the mounting complications. Eventually, on 25 November, the Élysée confirmed the suspension of the *Mistral* deal, due to the 'exceptional circumstances' in Ukraine.[68]

Two key considerations explain why the Hollande government tried to avoid cancelling the deal. Firstly, France's image as a reliable arms exporter was paramount to French defence policymakers. Just like during the Cold War, France sought to attract customers by depicting itself as a country that did not attach political conditions to arms sales and would not cease deliveries if a customer's political or military situation changed. More specifically, there were concerns that cancelling the *Mistral* deal with Russia would adversely affect negotiations with India for the sale of *Rafale* combat aircraft.[69] A second factor was financial penalties: in accordance with the contract Russia could not only ask for its payments for the two *Mistral* ships to be refunded but could also claim financial compensation for delayed delivery.

As for the economic considerations, they were less important in 2014–15 than they had been in 2009–11, before the deal was signed. The STX shipyard's problems had eased somewhat, with both of the *Mistral* vessels already having been built and the company also receiving new civilian orders.[70] It was also the case that the costs of cancelling the deal were covered by the state, not by the defence companies themselves.[71]

The reasons to suspend the *Mistral* deal, meanwhile, seemed stronger in 2014–15 than a few years previously. Again, the US and Eastern European countries were voicing their opposition. France came under pressure from the US during G7, G20 and NATO meetings in 2014, and Poland and the Baltic states were particularly vehement. Even Japan protested, on the grounds that Russia had indicated it would deploy the first *Mistral* close to the Kuril Islands.[72] Ukraine added its voice to the outpouring of concern.[73] Not only were France's allies unsettled by the continued possibility of Russia receiving the *Mistral*s, but the deal appeared to contradict its own foreign policy. For example, although President Hollande had been the first foreign head of state to recognise the Syrian opposition as the country's legitimate representatives, Russia would potentially be able to deploy the *Mistral*s in the Mediterranean in support of President Bashar al-Assad's forces.

Another factor in favour of the suspension of the *Mistral* sale was the prospect of securing other major arms contracts. Poland, for example, had announced a large-scale defence-procurement plan, and France was bidding to supply it with products including helicopters and air-defence systems. However, the Polish government had made clear that if France delivered the *Mistral*s to Russia, its equipment stood no chance of being selected.[74] Significantly, when Hollande began to backtrack on the deal in early September 2014, it was not only just before a NATO summit but also during the annual MSPO arms fair in Poland.

Favourable winds for French arms exporters

Although in 2014 it was the *Mistral* affair that grabbed the headlines, France achieved numerous arms-sales successes during Hollande's presidency. The year 2015 was particularly busy. Not only did Dassault Aviation sign a contract with Egypt for the sale of 24 *Rafale* combat aircraft, but Egypt also bought the two *Mistral* amphibious assault ships that had been built for

Russia, along with a FREMM frigate. A deal was signed with Qatar for another 24 *Rafales*, and then India announced its intention to buy 36 *Rafales*, with the contract eventually signed in 2016. There were sales of military helicopters to Kuwait (the *Caracal*) and to Uzbekistan (the *Cougar* and *Fennec*).

In the autumn of 2013, Saudi Arabia had placed orders for the modernisation of various types of frigate and oil tanker, and Singapore had procured *Aster* 30 missiles. French military satellites had been acquired in 2014 by Peru and the United Arab Emirates. Later, in April 2016, DCNS secured a €34bn (US$38bn) contract with Australia for the sale of 12 *Attack*-class submarines.

While the reorganisation of arms-export support might have played a role in securing those contracts, French defence firms also benefited from a favourable international context, particularly in the Middle East. Since the Arab Spring, the Sunni-led countries, including the Gulf states, had distanced themselves somewhat from the United States because Washington had neither prevented the overthrow of President Hosni Mubarak during the Egyptian revolution of 2011 nor, more importantly, intervened against Assad in Syria in 2013. Washington's willingness to reach a deal with Iran on the nuclear issue also met with Sunni disapproval. For Egypt and the United Arab Emirates, another bone of contention was that in the ongoing conflict in Libya, restrictions imposed by the US prevented them from using their US-supplied combat aircraft.[75]

France, meanwhile, adopted positions on some of these issues that seemed more in line with the interests of the Sunni-led countries. On Syria, France had been ready to intervene until the U-turn by the US. Throughout the Hollande presidency the French government maintained a hard line against Assad, insisting on his resignation. During the negotiations with Iran on its nuclear programme, France adopted a tougher position than the US, wanting stricter conditions for the lifting of sanctions. The Sunni-led countries were therefore looking more favourably on France than on the US,[76] and this created fertile ground for French arms sales in the region.

The Gulf Cooperation Council's invitation to President Hollande to attend its summit in May 2015 symbolised the close cooperation between the Gulf monarchies and France at the time. The French government was even reportedly considering intervening in Yemen alongside Saudi Arabia.[77] Since 2013, Saudi Arabia had become the world's leading client for French arms exports, accumulating more than €1.9bn (US$2.5bn) of purchases.[78] In 2013, for example, Thales obtained a €140 million (US$186m) contract for the maintenance of *Crotale* air-defence systems;[79] DCNS, Thales and MBDA signed the €1bn (US$1.3bn)-plus LEX (Life Extension *Sawari* 1) contract for the overhaul of frigates and oil tankers; DCNS agreed a €150m (US$199m) deal to modernise three other frigates (*Sawari* 2);[80] and MBDA agreed to supply the Saudi armed forces with VL-MICA, *Mistral* and *Storm Shadow* missiles.[81] In 2014, France was awarded a contract of up to US$3bn to equip the Lebanese armed forces as part of a Saudi Arabian aid package,[82] although Saudi Arabia itself has since taken the materiel because of fears in Riyadh about Iranian influence, through Hizbullah, over Lebanese affairs.[83] It was also reported that Saudi Arabia helped to finance Egypt's acquisition of the French *Rafale* combat aircraft and *Mistral* amphibious assault ships.[84] And Riyadh indicated that it might buy *Leclerc* tanks, *Rafale* combat aircraft and satellites after the 2017 French presidential election, although none of those deals have been signed.

During Hollande's presidency, a further boost to arms exports came from the deployment of French forces in military equipment operations overseas. France intervened in Mali in January 2013 to halt an offensive by Islamist and Tuareg groups from the north of the country (*Opération Serval*), and in the Central African Republic in December 2013 in response to fighting between pro-Islamic and pro-Christian militias (*Opération Sangaris*). In August 2014, *Opération Serval* was succeeded by *Opération Barkhane*, aimed at combating terrorist groups in the broader Sahel region. Under the name *Opération Chammal*, French combat aircraft were also part of the coalitions fighting the Islamic State, also known as ISIS or ISIL, in Iraq from September 2014 and in Syria from September 2015. These deployments, along with France's involvement in the intervention in Libya back in 2011, provided the *Rafale* combat aircraft and other French materiel with the label 'combat proven', enhancing its appeal to potential buyers.

The rapprochement between the US and the Gulf states since President Donald Trump's arrival in office appears to have narrowed the window of opportunity that French defence companies exploited for a number of years. Since the election of President Emmanuel Macron in May 2017, the most significant French arms sales have been to other European countries. Belgium's purchase of 60 *Jaguar* and 382 *Griffon* armoured vehicles was particularly important, partly because it led to the creation of a new export-support mechanism (similar to the United States' Foreign Military Sales mechanism), inaugurating a new model of government-to-government contracting that is expected to have a positive impact on other negotiations in future.[85] Beyond Europe, the most important negotiations since May 2017 have followed up on previous negotiations, such as sealing a deal for Australia's purchase of *Attack*-class submarines and taking further orders for *Rafale* combat aircraft from Qatar and Egypt.

The lack of response from Macron's government to mounting criticism over arms sales to countries involved in the war in Yemen – primarily Saudi Arabia and the United Arab Emirates – suggests that the French arms-export doctrine is being maintained by the current president. Despite the war, Macron announced a deal for two *Gowind* corvettes with the United Arab Emirates in November 2017,[86] while deliveries of CAESAR howitzers to Saudi Arabia continue.[87]

A persistent arms-export doctrine

Three decades after the end of the Cold War, the rationale that legitimises France's arms-export policy remains in place. No anti-arms-trade actor – whether in the bureaucratic, civil or political arena – has yet managed to dent it. According to this doctrine, arms sales are indispensable to French sovereignty because domestic orders are not sufficient to sustain the broad range of independent, technologically advanced defence companies whose products make France sovereign in the security realm. The doctrine has been structurally reinforced to the extent that it will be difficult for any French government to break its path dependence.

Firstly, the unquestioned support for arms exports derives from the entrenched notion of 'strategic autonomy' in French foreign and defence policy. This concept still drives decision-making in most aspects of French foreign affairs. When President Charles de Gaulle returned to power in 1958 and founded the Fifth Republic, he insisted that France should be independent from the two superpowers dominating the Cold War – and for this posture to be credible, the country required an autonomous capacity to build weapons systems for the needs of its armed forces. Arms sales sustained an independent defence industry, which in turn sustained the French independent posture. As a shortcut, success in the arms trade became a symbol of France's capacity to defend itself – or the 'business model of our sovereignty', as the country's defence minister, Florence Parly, put it in 2018.[1] During the Cold War, moreover, France's independent posture became a selling point for its arms exports. It could make the case to prospective customers that buying French meant buying neither from the United States nor the Soviet Union, and would therefore help tilt the world towards multipolarity. France's arms-export policy developed *tous azimuts*,[2] and in the process it became more difficult to question.

Secondly, this policy led to the creation of bureaucratic structures and processes to support its implementation. This was embodied in particular by the export-support structures of the Ministry of Defence's arms-procurement department, the Direction générale de l'armement (DGA). Outside government, semi-public organisations known as *Offices* were in charge of helping state-owned arms manufacturers promote their products in foreign markets, particularly in the Middle East. The bias towards supporting arms exports also infused the export-control processes, which, despite applying rigorous rules and procedures, was nonetheless embedded in a broader pro-export environment.

Thirdly, French arms-export policy should be understood in the context of weak checks on the executive in the country's semi-presidential political system, in which the powers of the legislature are limited. Foreign and defence policy remains the *domaine réservé* of the president, and legislators have limited means to scrutinise or challenge presidential decisions. This applies in particular to arms exports. Prior to 2000 there was no formal reporting of arms exports to parliament, and since then parliamentarians have shown little interest in the annual report the government has provided. In a recent television documentary, a La République En Marche (LREM) deputy admitted he had not read the report even though he was a member of the National Assembly's defence committee.[3] Furthermore, the French electoral system tends to produce large, stable majorities in parliament, reducing the ability of the smaller parties – which include those that are most critical of the arms trade – to influence policymaking. And the legislative and policymaking processes also leave little space for civil-society actors to exert influence. Combined, these factors give the executive and the bureaucracy a largely free hand in the sphere of arms exports.

However, these structural realities were challenged at the end of the Cold War. Change in the international system upended the traditional markets where French defence-industrial entities sold their products. Previously, the Soviet Union did not sell arms to the West and the United States did not sell arms to the East, affording France some room for manoeuvre. With the end of the Cold War the arms trade became increasingly competitive. Over time, new suppliers emerged, which further intensified competition. France's arms exporters also lost one of their selling points, namely that buying French meant not aligning with one of the two superpowers.

At the time, new multilateral agreements were being negotiated to introduce more regulation and control into the arms trade. From the 1990s onwards, several multinational forums began to discuss and adopt treaties and conventions in this regard. These included the OECD Convention on Combating Bribery of Foreign Public Officials in International Business Transactions (or OECD Anti-Bribery Convention), which affected how French arms exporters conducted their business, all the way to the more recent Arms Trade Treaty, which was adopted by the United Nations in 2013 and entered into force in 2014.

Europe-wide, the defence industry had to adapt to changing circumstances, facing lower defence budgets, cancellations and reductions of weapons programmes at home, and more competition abroad. The industry restructured, with European consolidation occurring in the aerospace and missile sectors, and, in France as elsewhere, partial privatisation. In the EU, France also had to adapt to emerging regulations on arms-export controls, aimed at facilitating intra-European armaments cooperation for the new European-wide defence groups and at satisfying those with a more restrictive approach to extra-EU exports.

These new trends meant – theoretically – that France could no longer conduct its export policy as it had done in the past. It had to fight to retain existing customers, win new ones, work within a transformed industrial landscape, and navigate a global system that was beginning to embrace regulation and control.

Yet despite these pressures, under the successive presidencies of Jacques Chirac, Nicolas Sarkozy and François Hollande, the fundamental tenets of the policy were little changed – and Emmanuel Macron, so far, has steered a similar course. French arms-export policy today still operates under a *dirigiste* approach. In the early 1990s, in the context of tougher competition in the global market, there were attempts to initiate a relative state retrenchment from arms-sales support. Following liberalisation of the defence-industrial sector, state actors took a step back and private companies became more proactive in marketing their arms. The DGA's export-promotion department, the Direction du développement international (DI), was weakened in the 1990s, and the *Offices* were gradually dismantled. However, by the mid-2000s, this new dispensation was regarded as inefficient, and there were calls to revive state support. Under Sarkozy, new state institutions were created to support arms exports. However, the core of policy decision-making was at the Élysée, which impeded proper cross-bureaucratic coordination. This system was changed again under the Hollande presidency. Defence minister Jean-Yves Le Drian rebalanced the division of labour between the state and the private sector. State actors were responsible for strategic partnerships with potential customers, while the companies focused on industrial and technical negotiations.

In addition to this *dirigiste* approach to arms-export support, French governments have responded to increased competition in the global arms market by seeking to simplify the export-control system and streamline the processes by which defence companies receive authorisation to export. This trend has been almost entirely uninterrupted throughout the post-Cold War era. The elaborate bureaucratic export-control process involves a number of departments that are meticulous in their approach to issuing licences. However, the absence of political debate about the direction of France's arms-export policy means that to a large extent the bureaucracy has been allowed to become the arbiter of export control. This situation has gradually led the defence establishment – politicians and civil servants alike – to conflate two aspects of the arms-export system: the rigorous bureaucratic procedures, and the policy orientation. Between 1997 and 2002 the Socialist government adopted a more restrictive approach, albeit only by making the bureaucratic process more complex. There was no significant change in terms of outcomes because the underlying doctrine went unchallenged.

French arms-export policy as an obstacle to European defence cooperation

At the beginning of the 2020s, however, the doctrine is now facing new challenges. If France clings to it, defence policy might not be able to adapt to the new international society which is emerging. Given two slow developments – the efforts to regulate the arms market, and the integration of European countries' defence-industrial bases – and the pro-European vocation of President Macron, a measure of change might be necessary.

The regulatory dynamic has stepped up with the adoption of the Arms Trade Treaty (ATT). It has empowered non-governmental organisations (NGOs) in Europe to argue for a more restrictive approach towards the arms trade, especially because European states have armed participants in the war in Yemen since 2015, with dramatic humanitarian consequences. In February 2016 the European Parliament voted to impose an arms embargo against Saudi Arabia. This demand was not legally binding, but a number of countries have stopped selling arms to Riyadh, including Finland, Germany, the Netherlands and Norway. Sweden in April 2018 updated its arms-export-control guidelines to prohibit sales to non-democratic states. Even states that are yet to follow this route are debating it. In the United Kingdom, at the end of 2016, MPs recommended that the Foreign and Commonwealth Office suspend export licences for weapons that could be used in the war in Yemen.[4] British NGOs have attempted legal action against UK arms transfers to Saudi Arabia, under the rules of the ATT. In June 2019 the Court of Appeal ruled that, in granting licences for exports of arms to Saudi Arabia, the British government had not sufficiently taken into account violations of international humanitarian law in the war in Yemen.[5] This prompted the UK government to review its export-control process; it also considered appealing the judgment, but in the interim stated that it would not grant any new licences for exports to Saudi Arabia and its coalition partners (Bahrain, Egypt, Kuwait and the United Arab Emirates) of British arms that might be used in Yemen.[6] Although the government has since recognised that there were 'inadvertent breaches'[7] of the court order, the legal challenge in the UK has inspired campaigners elsewhere, such as the Rete Italiana per il Disarmo in Italy.[8] France now appears isolated in Europe, when some of its most important partners in armaments programmes have a more restrictive stance, albeit for differing reasons.

This renewed contestation is now perhaps influencing the debate in France. French NGOs have adopted a similar tactic to their British counterparts and started to question the legality of French arms sales to Saudi Arabia and the United Arab Emirates in the context of the war in Yemen, notably with regard to the ATT.[9] As of December 2019, a parliamentary fact-finding mission[10] was still in progress after Sébastien Nadot, a former LREM deputy in the National Assembly, demanded an investigation into French arms sales to countries involved in the war in Yemen. Nadot had in fact wanted a full parliamentary inquiry, but LREM, which currently controls the National Assembly, refused to go that far. Media pressure, meanwhile, has continued unabated, with the press publishing leaked military-intelligence documents discussing the possible use of French-made weapons in Yemen.[11]

However, the media and public opinion might not be the most potent factor that will push the French defence establishment to adjust its long-standing approach to arms exports. The strongest attacks on the doctrine might actually come from within, as it now appears to conflict with President Macron's strongly pro-European policies. At the European Union level, Permanent Structured Cooperation (PESCO) and the European Defence Fund (EDF) have been established. Outside the institutions of the EU, France has launched the European Intervention Initiative (EI2) in cooperation with ten other countries. PESCO and the EDF could pave the way for a greater number of trans-European armaments programmes. The EDF has also opened the door to new thinking within EU institutions about their potential role in arms-export control in the medium term. Indeed, EDF projects will be funded in part by the EU and in part by national governments. This raises the question of whether the European Commission, through its new Directorate General for Defence, should have a say in deciding which countries EDF-funded equipment will be exported to.

As of December 2019, the draft regulation for the EDF states that it 'shall not affect the discretion of Member States as regards policy on the export of defence-related products'.[12] However, European cooperation on defence exports will become even more important in the near future. If there is a growing number of joint programmes, then European states will need to agree on common export policies. Additionally, recent years have seen industrial consolidation across Europe – for example institutional rapprochement between Krauss-Maffei Wegmann and Nexter, and between Naval Group and Fincantieri – as well as the launch of new armaments projects such as the EuroMALE uninhabited aerial vehicle. France and Germany have announced new projects in several domains, notably a Future Combat Air System (FCAS) and a new Main Ground Combat System (MGCS). Although these are unlikely to enter service until the 2030s, such projects require the partner countries to agree now on how they will approach future arms-export opportunities.

Indeed, divergences on export controls jeopardise current efforts to deepen and rationalise the defence-industrial land-scape in Europe. The war in Yemen has divided European states on the question of arms transfers.[13] In some states, political parties oppose arms sales to countries at war or where human-rights violations occur. This is the case of the Green Party in Sweden and the Social Democratic Party (SPD) in Germany, which campaigned on this issue during recent elections.[14]

France has a particular problem with Germany in this sphere. In 2012 the German government blocked exports to Saudi Arabia by Nexter, France's main land-weapons manufacturer.[15] In 2014 and 2015 the French media reported that Germany had blocked sales to Qatar by MBDA Systems and to Uzbekistan by Airbus.[16] More recently, Berlin has reportedly blocked exports to Saudi Arabia for a number of joint programmes with France and other countries, such as the Eurofighter *Typhoon*, *Meteor* missiles, A330 tanker aircraft, the H145 helicopter and the CASA C295 transport aircraft.[17] France's defence minister, Florence Parly, acknowledges that this has become a political issue and needs to be solved.[18]

In effect, the 1972 Franco-German agreement on arms exports has been rendered obsolete. The Schmidt–Debré letter was signed by the German and French defence ministers, Helmut Schmidt and Michel Debré, in 1971 and 1972 respectively. This political agreement dealt specifically with the issue of arms exports to third countries in the case of joint weapons programmes.[19] It set out a list of six weapons programmes in development at the time, but also applied to 'future cooperation projects'. Today there is dissatisfaction on both sides with the agreement. While some in France are calling for 'German-free' arms production, in order to circumvent Germany's more restrictive export policy, this would be completely at odds with the pro-European approach of President Macron and his government. If Macron maintains his pro-European stance, including in the defence field, he will have to spend considerable political capital to direct French arms-export policy away from the course it has followed since the 1960s. So far, France has tended to blame Germany for export disputes. However, it could be argued that France's inflexibility and the lack of political debate on arms sales have become obstacles to deeper defence cooperation with its main European partner. Indeed, its traditional arms-export doctrine is now preventing France from taking bolder steps in its desire to build European defence.

Denting the doctrine

There are signs that times might be changing. In October 2019, France and Germany reached an agreement on export rules for joint armaments programmes.[20] Following the bilateral Aix-la-Chapelle/Aachen Treaty of January 2019, the two countries agreed that, for intergovernmental programmes and their subsystems, and for defence products linked to industrial cooperation, any export veto should be 'exceptional' – as was already set out in the 1972 agreement. The novel aspect of the October 2019 agreement is the creation of a 'de minimis' principle for components and parts that are not covered by the two previous categories of cooperation. This principle applies when the share of products destined for integration in the other party's weapons system is under 20% of the value of the final system to be exported. In such instances, export authorisations should be granted without delay, unless exceptional circumstances apply. Finally, the agreement also created a 'permanent committee' for mutual consultation on these issues. Another indication of a possible shift in French arms-export policy was the decision to stop granting licences for arms exports to Turkey following its invasion of northern Syria in October 2019. Eight other European countries (the Czech Republic, Finland, Germany, Italy, the Netherlands, Spain, Sweden and the UK) made a similar move, as too did Canada.[21]

However, it is too early to say whether recent developments amount to a transformational shift in the French approach to exporting materiel. It will be difficult to change the doctrine until France integrates alternative voices in the formulation and implementation of its arms-export policy, which is still largely in the hands of a closed-door administrative system.

This would entail notably more parliamentary control, which for now is very limited. The challenge is to move arms-sales policy beyond the bureaucracy and into the realm of politics. A parliamentary commission could be brought into the CIEEMG export-control process, and parliament could produce its own annual report on arms exports – either initiative would give parliamentarians a greater chance of controlling the executive, and also better inform the wider public on arms-sales issues. More broadly, such moves would allow parliamentarians to consider which states France sees as its long-term partners, and to what extent arms sales should be a tool to build strategic partnerships. But for deeper change, the focus would have to move away from arms-deals successes and more towards cooperation with European partners, which has too often been regarded as entailing undesirable concessions. This applies not only to how the media portrays arms exports but also to strategic communication on the part of the government and to the way in which civil servants are encouraged to carry out their work within the defence bureaucracy. For instance, the annual report to parliament on arms exports could place greater emphasis on joint projects, which would help establish arms-cooperation policy as an important dimension of arms-export policy.

Looking outside the domestic arena, building consensus with European partners appears to be increasingly important. Germany is calling for further harmonisation of decision-making on EU export controls – but French attachment to national export controls is still clear. A stronger European regime for arms-export control could be a middle ground between the two positions. European discussions must be extended beyond the bureaucracies that are in charge of export-control processes, so as to include political decision-makers. At the EU level, such discussions could be conducted by members of the European Parliament, but in a way that ensures national parliaments are also involved. On a bilateral level, the newly established Franco-German Parliamentary Assembly could be a forum for building greater trust between the two countries on arms-sales issues, and talks between French and German political parties could also provide a way forward. A more integrated European approach would offer many opportunities. For industry, it would reduce uncertainty and also lower compliance costs. A unified approach would simplify processes and avoid the current divergence between different countries' export-control policies. For states, it would diminish risks of 'licence shopping', when defence companies move some of their operations to countries where export-control rules are less strict. However, for deeper European cooperation to take place, France's traditional arms-export doctrine needs to be put aside. More than 60 years after the doctrine began to take hold, it is time for a change.

APPENDIX

List of interviews

The list below contains all the interviews that served as sources for information in the book, indicating the date when each interview was conducted and the interviewee's position at the time.

Interview	Date	Interviewee
Interview 1	2 May 2014	Banker
Interview 2	4 March 2013	Researcher
Interview 3	22 April 2013	Researcher
Interview 4	25 April 2013	Researcher
Interview 5	30 January 2014	Researcher
Interview 6	13 February 2015	Researcher
Interview 7	29 April 2015	Researcher
Interview 8	7 May 2015	Researcher
Interview 9	15 October 2014	COFACE executive
Interview 10	27 March 2013	Defence-industry executive
Interview 11	9 April 2013	Defence-industry executive
Interview 12	24 April 2013	Defence-industry executive
Interview 13	24 April 2013	Defence-industry executive

Interview 14	7 May 2013	Defence-industry executive
Interview 15	4 June 2013	Defence-industry executive
Interview 16	21 June 2013	Defence-industry executive
Interview 17	1 July 2013	Defence-industry executive
Interview 18	12 July 2013	Defence-industry executive
Interview 19	15 July 2013	Defence-industry executive
Interview 20	17 July 2013	Defence-industry executive
Interview 21	27 August 2013	Defence-industry executive
Interview 22	27 August 2013	Defence-industry executive
Interview 23	17 March 2014	Defence-industry executive
Interview 24	17 April 2014	Defence-industry executive
Interview 25	17 April 2014	Defence-industry executive
Interview 26	30 April 2014	Defence-industry executive
Interview 27	30 September 2014	Defence-industry executive
Interview 28	3 October 2014	Defence-industry executive
Interview 29	6 October 2014	Defence-industry executive
Interview 30	10 October 2014	Defence-industry executive
Interview 31	13 October 2014	Defence-industry executive
Interview 32	20 March 2015	Defence-industry executive
Interview 33	20 January 2013	Ministry of Foreign Affairs official
Interview 34	5 June 2013	Ministry of Foreign Affairs official
Interview 35	11 June 2013	Ministry of Foreign Affairs official
Interview 36	19 June 2013	Ministry of Foreign Affairs official
Interview 37	19 June 2013	Ministry of Foreign Affairs official
Interview 38	3 July 2013	Ministry of Foreign Affairs official
Interview 39	23 October 2014	Ministry of Foreign Affairs official
Interview 40	4 May 2015	Ministry of Foreign Affairs official
Interview 41	19 March 2013	Ministry of Defence official (DGA)
Interview 42	23 March 2013	Ministry of Defence official (DGA)
Interview 43	23 March 2013	Ministry of Defence official (EMA)
Interview 44	25 March 2013	Ministry of Defence official (DAS)

Interview 45	11 April 2013	Ministry of Defence official (DGA)
Interview 46	11 April 2013	Defence-industry executive
Interview 47	16 April 2013	Ministry of Defence official (DGA)
Interview 48	30 April 2013	Ministry of Defence official (DGA)
Interview 49	3 May 2013	Ministry of Defence official (DGA)
Interview 50	3 May 2013	Ministry of Defence official (DGA)
Interview 51	14 May 2013	Ministry of Defence official (DGA)
Interview 52	31 May 2013	Ministry of Defence official (DGA)
Interview 53	4 June 2013	Ministry of Defence official (DGA)
Interview 54	7 June 2013	Ministry of Defence official (EMA)
Interview 55	10 June 2013	Ministry of Defence official (DGA)
Interview 56	13 June 2013	Ministry of Defence official (DGA)
Interview 57	28 June 2013	Ministry of Defence official (DGA)
Interview 58	3 July 2013	Ministry of Defence official (DGA)
Interview 59	3 July 2013	Ministry of Defence official (DGA)
Interview 60	7 July 2013	Ministry of Defence official (DGA)
Interview 61	8 July 2013	Ministry of Defence official (legal department)
Interview 62	16 July 2013	Ministry of Defence official (armaments attaché)
Interview 63	18 July 2013	Ministry of Defence official (DGA)
Interview 64	22 July 2013	Ministry of Defence official (DAS)
Interview 65	28 August 2013	Ministry of Defence official (DGA)
Interview 66	23 April 2014	Ministry of Defence official (EMA)
Interview 67	26 April 2014	Ministry of Defence official (DGA)
Interview 68	9 May 2014	Ministry of Defence official (DGA)
Interview 69	16 June 2014	Ministry of Defence official (DGA)
Interview 70	16 September 2014	Ministry of Defence official (EMA)
Interview 71	1 October 2014	Ministry of Defence official (DGA)
Interview 72	16 October 2014	Ministry of Defence official (DGA)
Interview 73	21 October 2014	Ministry of Defence official (DAS)
Interview 74	11 October 2012	Ministry of the Economy official
Interview 75	9 July 2013	Ministry of the Economy official

Interview 76	23 April 2013	NGO activist
Interview 77	12 June 2013	NGO activist
Interview 78	20 March 2013	Former Minister of Defence
Interview 79	3 June 2013	Deputy in National Assembly
Interview 80	10 June 2013	Special adviser to the Minister of Defence
Interview 81	2 July 2013	Political appointee (*cabinet* of Minister of Defence)
Interview 82	24 July 2013	Political appointee (*cabinet* of Minister of Defence)
Interview 83	20 December 2013	Political appointee (*cabinet* of Minister of Defence)
Interview 84	27 January 2013	Political appointee (*cabinet* of Minister of Defence)
Interview 85	19 March 2014	Political appointee (*cabinet* of Minister of Defence)
Interview 86	30 May 2013	SGDSN official
Interview 87	7 June 2013	SGDSN official
Interview 88	18 June 2013	SGDSN official
Interview 89	18 July 2013	SGDSN official
Interview 90	18 December 2013	SGDSN official
Interview 91	19 November 2018	Deputy in National Assembly

Introduction

1 Thomas Wieder, 'Rentrée du PS: qui est le "Melon d'or" de l'année?', *Le Monde*, 23 August 2013, https://www.lemonde.fr/politique/article/2013/08/23/rentree-du-ps-qui-est-le-melon-d-or-de-l-annee_3465733_823448.html.

2 Laurent Lagneau, 'La mise au point du Pdg de Dassault Aviation', *Zone militaire Opex 360*, 21 October 2013, http://www.opex360.com/2013/10/21/la-mise-au-point-du-pdg-de-dassaut-aviation/.

3 'Transformation de la DGA', discours de Florence Parly, ministre des Armées, 5 July 2018, https://www.defense.gouv.fr/salle-de-presse/discours/discours-de-florence-parly/discours_balard_05-07-2018_transformation_dga.

4 Hennie van Vuuren, *Apartheid Guns and Money: A Tale of Profit* (London: Hurst, 2018).

5 Mike Thomson, 'How France helped both sides in the Falklands War', BBC News, 6 March 2012, https://www.bbc.co.uk/news/magazine-17256975.

6 'Giraud announces tighter control of arms exports', *Jane's Defence Weekly*, 14 November 1988, p. 1096.

7 *Ibid.*, p. 1096.

8 Samy Cohen, *La défaite des généraux. Le pouvoir politique et l'armée sous la Vè République* (Paris: Fayard, 1994), p. 169.

9 'Le rapport Barba fournit des pistes pour la recherche des bénéficiaires des commissions', *Le Monde*, 3 November 1987.

10 Kim Willsher, '"Karachi affair": six on trial in France over arms-sales scandal', *Guardian*, 7 October 2019, https://www.theguardian.com/world/2019/oct/07/french-politicians-to-face-trial-in-arms-sales-corruption-case.

11 Stockholm International Peace Research Institute, 'The Financial Value of the Global Arms Trade', https://www.sipri.org/databases/financial-value-global-arms-trade.

12 Ministère des Armées, Rapport au Parlement sur les exportations d'armement de la France 2019, June 2019, p. 103, https://www.defense.gouv.fr/content/download/559159/9678968/RAP%20 2019-Parties%201-2-3%2BAnnexes.pdf.

Chapter One

1. 'Boom time for French armaments – thanks to the killer Mirage', *Standard*, 10 February 1971.

2. Jean-Paul Hébert, *Production d'armement. Mutation du système français* (Paris: La documentation française, 1995), p. 13.

3. Edward A. Kolodziej, *Making and Marketing Arms: The French Experience and Its Implications for the International System* (Princeton, NJ: Princeton University Press, 1987), p. 83.

4. *Ibid.*, p. 138.

5. Sénat, Compte-rendu intégral, 2ème séance du 17 November 1961, 1ère session ordinaire de 1961–1962, 'Loi de finances pour 1962 – Suite de la discussion d'un projet de loi' – see speeches by Jacques Soufflet (p. 1584) and André Méric (p. 1591), http://www.senat.fr/comptes-rendus-seances/5eme/pdf/1961/11/s19611117_2_1573_1609.pdf.

6. Assemblée Nationale, Compte-rendu intégral, 1ère séance du 24 octobre 1967, 1ère session ordinaire de 1967–68, 'Loi de finances pour 1968 – Suite de la discussion d'un projet de loi' – see speeches by M. Jean-Paul Palewski (p. 4024) and Jacques Hébert (p. 4030), http://archives.assemblee-nationale.fr/3/cri/1967-1968-ordinaire1/023.pdf.

7. Jean-Pierre Mithois, 'France: Les exportations de matériels de guerre représentent 13% de celles de l'industrie mécanique', *Le Figaro*, 10 February 1970.

8. 'Boom time for French armaments - thanks to the killer Mirage'. For other, similar quotes from Debré, see: 'L'armement en France: 5% de nos exportations, 270 000 salariés', *Paris Presse*, 24 January 1970; and Charles Hargrove, 'New Trend in French arms sales', *The Times*, 24 March 1970, p. 22.

9. Speech by Charles Hernu, Minister of Defence, 5 February 1983, in Pierre Dussauge and Christophe Cornu, *L'industrie française de l'armement. Coopérations, restructurations et intégrations européennes* (2nd ed.) (Paris: Economica, 1998), pp. 101–02.

10. McKinsey & Co., 'Les exportations françaises d'armement: 40 000 emplois dans nos régions', Étude d'impact réalisée para le ministère de la Défense et le CIDEF, September 2014, https://www.defense.gouv.fr/espanol/actualites/articles/exportations-francaises-d-armement-40-000-emplois-dans-nos-regions.

11. Lettre n°13 790 du 10 avril 1970 – Service historique de la défense, Centre des archives de l'armement et du personnel civil, Châtellerault.

12. Memorandum sent from the minister's *cabinet* to other departments in the Ministry of Defence, 12 April 1976.

13. Livre Blanc sur la Défense Nationale, Tome 1, 1972, p. 54.

14. 'M. Chirac: les ventes d'armes procurent du travail à de nombreux ouvriers français', *Le Monde*, 15 January 1976, https://www.lemonde.fr/archives/article/1976/01/15/m-chirac-les-ventes-d-armes-procurent-du-travail-a-de-nombreux-ouvriers-francais_2956528_1819218.html.

15. 'Ventes d'armes: le ministre français de la Défense favorable à une nouvelle conception', *Afrique Défense*, June 1982, p. 28.

16. Jacques Isnard, 'La France veut accroître ses exportations d'armes', *Le Monde*, 19 January 1984, https://www.lemonde.fr/archives/article/1984/01/19/la-france-veut-accroitre-ses-exportations-d-armes_3001643_1819218.html.

17 Patrick Piernaz, 'Armement. Les secrets du tir français', *L'Usine Nouvelle*, 20 April 1985, pp. 36–37.

18 François Chesnais and Claude Serfati, *L'armement en France. Genèse, ampleur et coût d'une industrie* (Paris: Nathan, 1992), p. 161.

19 Alexandra Schwartzbrod, 'Les offices d'armement organisent leur défense', *Les Echos*, 5 June 1992, p. 16, https://www.lesechos.fr/1992/06/les-offices-darmement-organisent-leur-defense-927424.

20 COFACE, 'COFACE transfère la gestion des garanties publiques à l'export à Bpifrance', 2 January 2017, http://www.coface.com/fr/Actualites-Publications/Actualites/Coface-transfere-la-gestion-des-garanties-publiques-a-l-export-a-Bpifrance.

21 Direction Generale de l'Armement (DGA), IXARM le portail de l'armement, 'Article 90', 18 April 2018, https://www.ixarm.com/fr/soutien-financier-aux-exportations.

22 Interview 19.

23 Stéphane Reb, 'Mobiliser les acteurs du développement des exportations de défense', pp. 109–13, in 'Economie de défense', *Les Cahiers de la Revue Défense Nationale/Observatoire économique de la défense*, Spring 2013, p. 111.

24 Interview 66.

25 *Ibid.*

26 François Frison-Roche, 'Des savoirs experts au service de la Défense', in Philippe Bezes et al. (eds), *L'État à l'épreuve des sciences sociales. La fonction recherche in les administrations sous la Ve République* (Paris: La Découverte, 2005), pp. 295–315.

27 Interview 82.

28 *Ibid.*

29 Interview 66.

30 *Ibid.*

31 Assemblée Nationale, Audition de Mme Alice Guitton, directrice générale des relations internationales et de la stratégie, sur le projet de loi de finances pour 2019, Commission de la défense nationale et des forces armées, Compte-rendu 6, 10 October 2018, http://www.assemblee-nationale.fr/15/cr-cdef/18-19/c1819006.asp.

32 'La réforme de la Direction générale de l'armement en point de mire du ministère', RFI, 6 July 2018, http://www.rfi.fr/france/20180706-reforme-direction-generale-armement-dga-point-mire-ministere.

33 Interview 53.

34 Interview 38.

35 Interview 35.

36 Interview 38.

37 Interview 75.

38 *Ibid.*

39 Interview 83.

40 Interviews 49 and 50.

41 Interview 87.

42 Interview 68.

43 'Mistral Blows All Way to Moscow', *Intelligence Online*, 17 September 2009, https://www.intelligenceonline.com/corporate-intelligence/2009/09/17/mistral-blows-all-way-to-moscow,69657230-art.

44 Interview 88.

45 Interview 82.

46 Interview 87.

47 Interview 39.

48 Interview 53.

49 Interview 81.

50 Interview 85.

51 Jean Guisnel, 'Armement: la France, supermarché de l'Arabie Saoudite', *Le Point*, 20 March 2017, http://www.lepoint.fr/editos-du-point/jean-guisnel/armement-la-france-supermarche-de-l-arabie-saoudite-20-03-2017-2113291_53.php; 'Comment Macron soutient les

ventes d'armes à l'Arabie saoudite', *Challenges*, 22 February 2018, https://www.challenges.fr/economie/comment-macron-soutient-les-ventes-d-armes-a-l-arabie-saoudite_569274.

52 Renaud Bellais, *Production d'armes et puissance des nations* (Paris: L'Harmattan, 1999).

53 Martin Lundmark, 'To be or not to be – the integration and the non-integration of the French defence industry', The FIND Programme, FOI (Swedish Defence Research Agency), 2004, p. 15, https://www.foi.se/rest-api/report/FOI-R--1291--SE.

54 Samy Cohen, *La défaite des généraux. Le pouvoir politique et l'armée sous la Vè République* (Paris: Fayard, 1994), p. 241.

55 Jacques Fontanel and Jean-Paul Hébert, 'The end of the "French grandeur policy"', *Defence and Peace Economics*, vol. 8, no. 1, 1997, pp. 37–55 , pp. 45–46.

56 Jean Joana, 'Armée et industrie de défense: cousinage nécessaire et liaisons incestueuses', *Pouvoirs*, vol. 125, no. 2, 2008, pp. 43–54, p. 47.

57 Marc R. DeVore and Moritz Weiss, 'Who's in the cockpit? The political economy of collaborative aircraft decisions', *Review of International Political Economy*, vol. 21, no. 2, 2014, pp. 497–533, pp. 507, 522, https://www.tandfonline.com/doi/pdf/10.1080/09692290.2013.787947?needAccess=true.

58 Pierre Muller, *Airbus ou l'ambition européenne. Logique d'État, logique de marché* (Paris: L'Harmattan/Commissariat général du Plan, 1989).

59 Laurent Giovachini, *L'armement français au XXème siècle. Une politique à l'épreuve de l'histoire* (Paris: Ellipses, Les Cahiers de l'Armement, 2000), p. 112.

60 William Genieys, *Le choix des armes: Théories, acteurs et politiques* (Paris: CNRS Editions, 2004).

61 Edward A. Kolodziej, *Making and Marketing Arms: The French Experience and Its Implications for the International System*, p. 295.

62 Interview 76.

63 Laurent Giovachini, *L'armement français au XXème siècle. Une politique à l'épreuve de l'histoire*, p. 101.

64 Interview 49.

65 Assemblée Nationale, Rapport d'information n°1271, déposé par la Mission d'information de la Commission de la Défense Nationale et des Forces armées et de la Commission des Affaires étrangères sur les opérations militaires menées par la France, d'autres pays et l'ONU au Rwanda entre 1990 et 1994, Président, M. Paul Quilès, Rapporteurs, MM. Pierre Brana et Bernard Cazeneuve, 15 December 1998, http://www.assemblee-nationale.fr/11/dossiers/rwanda/r1271.asp.

66 'Kazakhgate: Notre dossier complet', *La Libre Belgique*, https://www.lalibre.be/dossier/belgique/politique-belge/kazakhgate-notre-dossier-complet-5832d207cd70735194a585bb, accessed 22 January 2020; Martine Orange and Yann Philippin, 'The secret Kazakh bung worrying Airbus', Mediapart, 26 November 2017, https://www.mediapart.fr/en/journal/international/261117/secret-kazakh-bung-worrying-airbus.

67 Marie-Christine Kessler, *La politique étrangère de la France, Acteurs et processus* (Paris: Presses de Sciences Po, 1999), p. 23.

68 SGDSN, 'Assurer le secrétariat du conseil de défense et de sécurité nationale', http://www.sgdsn.gouv.fr/missions/assurer-le-secretariat-du-conseil-de-defense-et-de-securite-nationale/.

69 Samy Cohen, *La défaite des généraux. Le pouvoir politique et l'armée sous la Vè République*, p. 263.

70 Interview 76.

71 Bastien Irondelle et al., 'Evolution du contrôle parlementaire des forces armées en Europe', Études de l'IRSEM, n°22, Institut de Recherche Stratégique de l'École Militaire (IRSEM), Paris, 2012, pp. 68–69.

72 Ministère des Armées, 'Présentation du rapport d'exportation d'armement 2012 (video)', 11 September 2013, http://www.defense. gouv.fr/actualites/articles/presentation-du-rapport-d-exportation-d-armement-2012-video, last accessed 19 October 2014. The video is no longer on the Ministry of Defence's website but is available here: https://video-streaming.orange.fr/actu-politique/presentation-du-rapport-d-exportation-d-armement-2012-VID00000017KPy.html.

73 Interview 79.

74 Interview 73.

75 François Hollande, 'Perspectives de défense nationale', Revue Défense Nationale, vol. 749, April 2012, pp. 23–28.

76 See 'Mon projet pour la politique de défense de la France', discours de Benoît Hamon, Strasbourg, 23 March 2017, https://web.archive.org/web/20170327045155/https://www. benoithamon2017.fr/wp-content/uploads/2017/03/Benoit-Hamon-Monprojet-pour-la-politique-de-la-Defense-de-la-France.pdf.

77 Emmanuel Macron, 'La défense de la France: le prix de la liberté', Revue Défense Nationale, vol. 799, April 2017, pp. 43–48, http://www. defnat.com/revue-defense-nationale. php?cidrevue=815

78 'Groupe "Défense" – Fiches', 19 September 2016, released by WikiLeaks, https://wikileaks.org/macron-emails/emailid/50154; 'Arbitrages EM sur le programme Défense', 28 December 2016, released by WikiLeaks, https://wikileaks.org/macron-emails/emailid/55679; 'Notes pour EM', 24 October 2016, released by WikiLeaks, https://wikileaks.org/macron-emails/emailid/55103. See also a note on arms exports prepared for Macron's campaign team: Hervé Grandjean, 'Les exportations d'armement: état des lieux' [no date], released by WikiLeaks, https://wikileaks.org/macron-emails//fileid/50541/18127.

79 Assemblée Nationale, Proposition de résolution tendant à la création d'une commission d'enquête sur le respect des engagements internationaux de la France au regard des autorisations d'exportations d'armes, munitions, formations, services et assistance accordées ces trois dernières années aux belligérants du conflit au Yémen, 6 April 2018, http://www.assemblee-nationale. fr/15/propositions/pion0856.asp.

80 Interview 91.

81 France Info, 'Ventes d'armes à l'Arabie saoudite: "Je ne vois pas pourquoi ce serait interdit," explique Richard Ferrand, qui évoque "des relations de confiance"', 9 April 2018, https://twitter.com/franceinfo/status/983600013233278976/video/1; Europe 1, 'Les ventes d'armes à l'Arabie saoudite, "un intérêt clair" pour la France, selon Griveaux', 9 April 2018, http://www.europe1.fr/economie/les-ventes-darmes-a-larabie-saoudite-un-interet-clair-pour-la-france-selon-griveaux-3622352.

82 'Stopping Saudi arms sales over Khashoggi "pure demagoguery", Macron says', France 24, 26 October 2018, https://www.france24. com/en/20181026-stopping-saudi-arms-sales-over-khashoggi-pure-demagoguery-macron-says.

83 Europe Écologie Les Verts, 'Programme d'actions pour les temps qui viennent. Vivre mieux vers la société écologique', http://eelv.fr/wp-content/uploads/2012/03/projetpdf.pdf.

84 'Présidentielle: réponse de 8 candidats à l'Appel d'Amnesty International', 12 April 2012, https://web.archive.org/web/20160109174232/http://www.amnesty.fr/Informez-vous/Les-actus/Ameliorer-les-droits-humains-une-priorite-pour-quels-candidats-5163.

85 La France Insoumise, 'Une France indépendante au service de la paix', April 2017, p. 25, https://avenirencommun.fr/livret-garde-nationale-defense/.

86 Rassemblement Nationale, 'La défense et les armées au cœur du projet pour la France', April 2017, https://www.rassemblementnational.fr/pdf/A4_LIVRET_DEFENSE.pdf, p. 11.

Chapter Two

1 Aude-Emmanuelle Fleurant, 'Vers un changement structurel de l'économie de défense mondiale?', in *Quelles stratégies face aux mutations de l'économie de défense mondiale?*, Étude de l'IRSEM n°38, by Aude-Emmanuelle Fleurant, (Paris: Institut de recherches stratégiques de l'École Militaire, 2015), pp. 10–19, p. 17, https://www.irsem.fr/data/files/irsem/documents/document/file/1055/Etude_IRSEM_n38.pdf.

2 SIPRI Arms Transfers Database, 'Importer/exporter TIV tables', http://armstrade.sipri.org/armstrade/page/values.php. 'The bar graph shows annual totals and the line graph shows the five-year moving average (each data point in the line graph represents an average for the preceding five-year period). The SIPRI trend-indicator value (TIV) is a measure of the volume of international transfers of major arms'. Source: Pieter D. Wezeman, et al., 'Trends in International Arms Transfers, 2018', SIPRI Factsheet, March 2019, https://www.sipri.org/sites/default/files/2019-03/fs_1903_at_2018.pdf.

3 SIPRI Military Expenditure Database, http://www.sipri.org/research/armaments/milex/research/armaments/milex/milex_database. Data are in US$ million at constant 2016 prices and exchange rates, except for the last figure, which is in US$m at 2017 prices and exchange rates.

4 SIPRI Arms Transfers Database, 'Importer/exporter TIV tables'.

5 International Institute for Strategic Studies (IISS), *The Military Balance 2018* (London: Routledge, 2018); Lucie Beraud-Sudreau, 'European defence spending: the new consensus', *Military Balance* blog, 15 February 2018, https://www.iiss.org/blogs/military-balance/2018/02/european-defence-spending.

6 Aude-Emmanuelle Fleurant et al., 'Trends in International Arms Transfers, 2015', SIPRI Fact Sheet, 2016, p. 2, https://www.sipri.org/publications/2016/sipri-fact-sheets/

trends-international-arms-trans-fers-2015.

7 Emma Soubrier, 'Mirages of Power? From Sparkly Appearances to Empowered Apparatus, Evolving Trends and Implications of Arms Trade in Qatar and the UAE', in David DesRoches and Dania Thafer (eds), *The Arms Trade, Military Services and the Security Market in the Gulf* (Berlin: Gerlach Press, 2016).

8 SIPRI Arms Transfers Database, 'Importer/exporter TIV tables'. The USSR provided 60% of Iraq's arms imports during the same period.

9 See 'Address Before a Joint Session of the Congress on the Cessation of the Persian Gulf Conflict', speech delivered by George Bush, President of the United States, Washington DC, 6 March 1991, http://www.presidency. ucsb.edu/ws/index.php?pid=19364.

10 Daniel Colard, 'La diplomatie française du désarmement sous la Vè République: 1958–2000', in *Annuaire Français de Relations Internationales (AFRI)*, de Centre Thucidyde, (Paris: Centre Thucidyde, 2001), pp. 411–25, p. 420.

11 Organisation for Security and Co-Operation in Europe, 'Principles Governing Conventional Arms Transfers', 25 November 1993, http://www.osce. org/fsc/42313.

12 Battle tanks; armoured combat vehicles; large-calibre artillery systems; combat aircraft; attack helicopters; warships; missiles and missile launchers.

13 Paul Holtom, Lucie Béraud-Sudreau and Henning Weber, 'Reporting to the United Nations Register of Conventional Arms', SIPRI Fact Sheet, May 2011, p. 2, https://www.sipri.org/ publications/2011/sipri-fact-sheets/ reporting-united-nations-register-conventional-arms; Pieter Wezeman and Siemon Wezeman, 'The 2015 UN Register on Conventional Arms: Still Time to Improve', 18 September 2015, http://www.sipri.org/media/ expert-comments/wezeman-sept-2015.

14 Bjorn Hagelin et al., 'International arms transfers', in *SIPRI Yearbook 2002. Armaments, Disarmament and International Security* (Oxford: Oxford University Press, 2002), p. 401.

15 Hélène Masson, '3. L'industrie de défense européenne et les marchés d'Amérique du nord et d'Amérique latine: entre attractivité et maîtrise des risques', pp. 81–114, in Yves Bélanger et al., *Les mutations de l'industrie de défense: Regards croisés sur trois continents. Amérique du nord - Europe - Amérique du sud* (Paris: Institut de recherches stratégiques de l'École Militaire, 2012), p. 104.

16 House of Commons, Select Committee on Defence, 'UK/US Declaration of Principles', https://publications.parliament.uk/pa/cm200203/ cmselect/cmdfence/694/694we15.htm; United States Deparment of State, 'U.S.–UK Joint Statement on Defense Export Controls', 17 January 2001, https://1997-2001.state.gov/briefings/ statements/2001/ps010117g.html.

17 Interview 55.

18 Interview 17.

19 Hassan Meddah, 'La France veut s'affranchir des restrictions américaines d'exportation d'armes', *L'Usine Nouvelle*, 7 September 2018, https://www.usine-nouvelle.com/article/la-france-veut-s-affranchir-des-contraintes-americaines-pour-exporter-ses-armes.N738374.

20 Michel Cabirol, 'Réglementation ITAR: États-Unis, cet ami qui ne veut pas que du bien à la France', *La Tribune*, 23 April 2018, https://www.latribune.fr/ entreprises-finance/industrie/aeronautique-defense/reglementation-itar-etats-

unis-ces-amis-qui-ne-veulent-pas-que-du-bien-a-la-france-776226.html.

21 Michel Cabirol, 'Exportations: comment MBDA desserre le noeud coulant des États-Unis (ITAR)', *La Tribune*, 27 March 2019, https://www.latribune.fr/entreprises-finance/industrie/aeronautique-defense/exportations-comment-mbda-desserre-le-noeud-coulant-des-etats-unis-itar-812016.html.

22 'Startup's programmable microchips may resolve ITAR export woes', *Intelligence Online*, no. 804, 17 April 2018, https://www.intelligenceonline.com/surveillance--interception/2018/04/17/startup-s-programmable-microchips-may-resolve-itar-export-woes,108306990-art.

23 Foreign and Commonwealth Office, 'Framework Agreement Concerning Measures to Facilitate the Restructuring and Operation of European Defence Industry', 27 July 2000, https://www.gov.uk/government/publications/framework-agreement-concerning-measures-to-facilitate-the-restructuring-and-operation-of-the-european-defence-industry-farnborough-2772000.

24 Interview with a Swedish diplomat, November 2013.

25 Michael Brzoska, 'The Framework Agreement: Accountability Issues', *European Security*, vol. 12, no. 3–4, 2003, pp. 73–94, p. 88.

26 Burkard Schmitt, 'A Common European Export Policy for Defence and Dual-Use Items?', *Occasional Papers* (Institute for Security Studies), vol. 25, 2001, pp. 1–24, pp. 17, 21, https://www.iss.europa.eu/sites/default/files/EUISS-Files/occ025.pdf.

27 Council of the European Union, 'European Union Code of Conduct on Arms Exports', Brussels, 5 June 1998, http://www.poa-iss.org/RegionalOrganizations/EU/EU%20Code%20of%20Conduct%201998.pdf.

28 See Criterion Three, Council of the European Union, 'European Union Code of Conduct on Arms Exports', Brussels, 5 June 1998, http://www.poa-iss.org/RegionalOrganizations/EU/EU%20Code%20of%20Conduct%201998.pdf.

29 Mark Bromley, '10 years down the track – the EU Code of Conduct on Arms Exports', *European Security Review* (ISIS Europe), vol. 39, July 2008, pp. 1–5.

30 Ian Anthony, 'National Policies and Regional Agreements on Arms Exports'. *Disarmament Forum* (UNIDIR), vol. 2, no. 2, 2000, pp. 47–58, https://www.unidir.org/files/publications/pdfs/small-arms-control-the-need-for-coordination-en-361.pdf.

31 Anna Stavrianakis, *Taking aim at the arms trade. NGOs, Global Civil Society and the World Military Order* (London: Zed Books, 2010), p. 75.

32 Pierre Martinot, '1998–2008, un anniversaire en demi-teinte pour le Code de Conduite européen sur les exportations d'armements', Note d'Analyse, Groupe de recherche et d'information sur la paix et la sécurité (GRIP), Brussels, 2008, p. 4, https://www.grip.org/en/node/227.

33 European Union, European External Action Service Annual reports on arms exports, https://eeas.europa.eu/headquarters/headquarters-homepage_en/8472/Annual%20reports%20on%20arms%20exports.

34 'EU Proposes to End to China Arms Embargo', *Deutsche Welle*, 15 April 2004, https://www.dw.com/en/eu-proposes-end-to-china-arms-embargo/a-1170380;

Daniel Dombey, 'EU still wants to lift China arms ban', *Financial Times*, 18 April 2005, https://www.ft.com/content/a4001e54-addd-11d9-9c30-00000e2511c8.

35 Andrew Rettman, 'France blocking ban for EU code on arms exports', *EU Observer*, 18 January 2007, http://euobserver.com/defence/23296.

36 European Commission, Communication, 'The Challenges Facing the European Defence-Related Industry, a Contribution for Action at European Level', 24 January 1996, https://eur-lex.europa.eu/legal-content/EN/TXT/?uri=CELEX:51996DC0010.

37 European Commission, Communication from the Commission to the European Parliament, the Council, the European Economic and Social Committee and the Committee of the Regions, 'Implementing European Union Strategy on Defence-Related Industries', 4 December 1997, https://eur-lex.europa.eu/legal-content/EN/TXT/?qid=1580924728795&uri=CELEX:51997DC0583.

38 Sibylle Bauer, 'The Europeanisation of Arms Export Policies and its Impact on Democratic Accountability', PhD dissertation, Université Libre de Brussels/Freie Universität Berlin, 2003, p. 102.

39 Interview 13.

40 European Commission, Communication from the Commission to the European Parliament, the Council, the European Economic and Social Committee and the Committee of the Regions, 'A Strategy for a stronger and more competitive European defence industry', 5 December 2007, https://eur-lex.europa.eu/legal-content/EN/TXT/HTML/?uri=CELEX:52007DC0764&from=EN.

41 European Commission, Communication from the Commission to the European Parliament, the Council, the European Economic and Social Committee and the Committee of the Regions, 'European Defence – Industrial and Market Issues, Towards an EU Defence Equipment Policy', 11 March 2003, https://eur-lex.europa.eu/legal-content/EN/TXT/HTML/?uri=CELEX:52003DC0113&from=EN.

42 European Commission, Commission Staff Working Document, Accompanying document to the Proposal for a Directive of the European Parliament and of the Council on simplifying terms and conditions of transfers of defence-related products within the Community, Impact Assessment, Brussels, 5 December 2007, https://eur-lex.europa.eu/LexUriServ/LexUriServ.do?uri=CELEX:52007SC1593:EN:HTML.

43 UNISYS, 'Intra-Community Transfers of Defence Products', Final report of the study 'Assessment of Community initiatives related to intra-community transfers of defence products', carried out by Unisys for the European Commission, Brussels, February 2005, p. 6, https://www.yumpu.com/en/document/read/15607739/intra-community-transfers-of-defence-products-edis.

44 European Commission, Commission Staff Working Document, Accompanying document to the Proposal for a Directive of the European Parliament and of the Council on simplifying terms and conditions of transfers of defence-related products within the Community.

45 Council of the European Union, Proposal for a Directive of the European Parliament and of the Council on simplifying terms and conditions of transfers of defence-related products within the Community, Brussels, 14 December 2007, https://eur-lex.europa.eu/legal-content/EN/TXT/HTML/?uri=CELEX:52007PC0765&from=FR.

46 Christian Mölling, '2. Options for an EU regime on intra-Community transfers of defence goods', pp. 51–88, in Daniel Keohane (ed.), *Towards a European Defence Market*, Chaillot Papers, vol. 113 (Paris: Institute for Security Studies, 2008), p. 61, https://www.iss.europa.eu/content/towards-european-defence-market.

47 Interview 79.

48 Secrétariat général des Affaires européennes, Note à la Commission euro-péenne, Circulation intracommunau-taire des produits liés à la défense des États membres, p. 2.

49 *Ibid.*, p. 2.

50 Interview 89.

51 Sénat, Réunion de la délégation pour l'Union européenne, Politique étran-gère et de défense, Paquet défense (Textes E3740 et E3741), Communica-tion de M. Dider Boulaud, 6 February 2008, https://www.senat.fr/europe/r06022008.html.

Chapter Three

1 SIPRI Military Expenditure Database, http://www.sipri.org/research/arma-ments/milex/research/armaments/milex/milex_database.

2 Bastien Irondelle, '11. "Qui contrôle le nerf de la guerre?" Financement et politique de défense', pp. 491–523, in Philippe Bezes and Alexandre Siné (eds), *Gouverner (par) les finances publiques* (Paris: Presses de Sciences Po, 2011), p. 495.

3 SIPRI Arms Transfers Database, Importer/exporter TIV tables, http://armstrade.sipri.org/armstrade/page/values.php.

4 Jacques Isnard, 'La fronde des indus-triels de la défense', *Le Monde*, 9 November 1994, p. 25, https://www.lemonde.fr/archives/article/1994/11/09/la-fronde-des-industriels-de-la-de-fense-contraintes-de-supprimer-des-emplois-les-societes-d-armement-de-mandent-a-l-etat-de-renegocier-leurs-contrats_3851510_1819218.html.

5 Jacques Isnard, 'M. Gérard Hibon aban-donne la vice-présidence du groupe Aérospatiale. La "reverence" d'un vendeur d'armes', *Le Monde*, 16 October 1991, https://www.lemonde.fr/archives/article/1991/10/16/m-gerard-hibon-aban-donne-la-vice-presidence-du-groupe-aerospatiale-la-reverence-d-un-vendeur-d-armes_4034405_1819218.html.

6 Interview 65.

7 SIPRI Arms Transfers Database, Importer/exporter TIV tables.

8 SIPRI Arms Transfers Database, Trade Registers, http://armstrade.sipri.org/armstrade/page/trade_register.php.

9 Jacques Isnard, 'Les ventes d'armes de la France. L'arroseur arrosé', *Le Monde*, 25 January 1991, https://www.lemonde.fr/archives/article/1991/01/25/les-ventes-d-armes-de-la-france-l-ar-roseur-arrose_4015701_1819218.html; 'Les ventes d'armes de la France. L'ar-roseur arrosé', *Le Monde*, 25 January 1991, p. 7.

10 Assemblée Nationale, Proposition de résolution tendant à la création d'une

commission d'enquête sur les exportations de matériels d'armement et les prestations qui y sont directement liées, François Léotard, n°1908, 15 March 1991.

11 Bruno Barrillot and Belkacem Elomari, *Les Transferts d'armes de la France 1991–1995* (Lyon/Villeurbane: Observatoire des Transfers d'Armement/Editions Golias, 1995), p. 6.

12 Assemblée Nationale, Proposition de loi tendant à la création d'une délégation parlementaire des exportations de matériels de guerre, François Fillon, n°1756, 22 November 1990.

13 François d'Aubert et al., Assemblée Nationale, Proposition de résolution tendant à la création d'une commission de contrôle sur le service public de l'assurance-crédit et la Coface, n°1914, 21 March 1991.

14 Jacques Isnard, 'M. Joxe veut vendre des Mirage à Taiwan', *Le Monde*, 13 May 1992, p. 1, https://www.lemonde.fr/archives/article/1992/05/13/m-joxe-veut-vendre-des-mirage-a-taiwan-apres-l-echec-finlandais_3909183_1819218.html.

15 'Taiwan seeks more French equipment', *Interavia Air Letter*, no. 12,745, 17 May 1993.

16 Giovanni de Briganti, 'French Lobby Gulf States for Weapon Export Deals', *Defense News*, 6–12 November 1995, p. 6.

17 [Foreign Broadcast Information Service, FBIS] AFP, 'Saudi, French Defense Ministers Discuss Tank Contract', 27 July 1997; Jacques Isnard, 'Riyad pose des conditions à l'achat de chars français Leclerc', *Le Monde*, 22 June 2000, https://www.lemonde.fr/archives/article/2000/06/22/riyad-pose-des-conditions-a-l-achat-de-chars-francais-leclerc_3604564_1819218.html; 'Leclerc Still Stuck in the Sand', *Intel-*

ligence Online, no. 428, 25 April 2002, https://www.intelligenceonline.com/political-intelligence/2002/04/25/leclerc-still-stuck-in-the-sand,3653704-art.

18 Giovanni De Briganti, 'French Face Pressure to Lift Exports as Procurement Falls', *Defense News*, April 1997, p. 10, pp. 11–17.

19 Bruno Durieux, Rapport au Premier ministre, Mission de reflexion et de proposition sur la politique d'exportation, 31 March 1996, pp. 12–14, http://www.ladocumentationfrancaise.fr/rapports-publics/964082600/index.shtml.

20 *Ibid.*, pp. 29–30.

21 Olivier Provost, 'La France prête à donner des matériels pour soutenir l'exportation', *La Tribune*, 21 April 1997.

22 Ministère des Armées, Rapport au Parlement sur les exportations d'armement de la France, Résultats 1998, March 2000, p. 13, https://www.vie-publique.fr/sites/default/files/rapport/pdf/024000061.pdf.

23 Assemblée Nationale, Commission de la défense nationale et des forces armées, Rapport d'information sur le contrôle des exportations d'armement n°2334, présenté par Jean-Claude Sandrier, Christian Martin et Alain Veryet, 25 April 2000, p. 156, http://www.assemblee-nationale.fr/rap-info/i2334.asp.

24 Olivier Provost, 'Les exportations françaises d'armement se redressent', *La Tribune*, 11 September 1997.

25 Jean-Claude Trichet, 'Les matériels français exportés. Un fonds de commerce soigneusement entretenu', Défense & Armements, no. 29, April 1984, p. 59; Livre Blanc sur la Défense, 1994, p. 130, https://www.vie-publique.fr/sites/default/files/rapport/pdf/944048700.pdf; Olivier Provost,

'Exportations d'armement: Léotard veut l'aide des armées', *La Tribune*, 30 January 1995.

26 Arnaud Idiart and Virgile Delaboudinière, '5. France', pp. 127–58, in Yann Aubin and Arnaud Idiart (eds), *Export control law and regulations handbook: A practical guide to military and dual-use goods* (Alphen aan den Rijn: Kluwer Law International, 2007), p. 141.

27 Giovanni De Briganti, 'French Government Considers Moves to Boost Arms Exports', *Defense News*, 21–27 April 1997, p. 68.

28 Assemblée Nationale, Première session Ordinaire de 1986–1987, 67ème séance, Compte-rendu intégral, 1ère séance du mercredi 12 November 1986, pp. 6124–25, http://archives.assemblee-nationale.fr/8/cri/1986-1987-ordinaire1/067.pdf.

29 François Chesnais and Claude Serfati, *L'armement en France. Genèse, ampleur et coût d'une industrie* (Paris: Nathan, 1992), p. 184.

30 Alexandra Schwartzbrod, 'Industries d'armement: le rôle de l'État appelé à s'inverser', *Les Echos*, 8 December 1992, https://www.lesechos.fr/1992/12/industries-darmement-le-role-de-letat-appele-a-sinverser-937702.

31 Jean-Pierre Neu, 'Aéronautique: les industriels rêvent d'un soutien à l'américaine', *Les Echos*, 22 March 1995, https://www.lesechos.fr/1995/03/aeronautique-les-industriels-revent-dun-soutien-a-lamericaine-853563.

32 'Création d'une direction du Commerce international chez Dassault', *MedNews*, 26 June 1989, p. 5.

33 'Société de commerce pour les opérations export d'Aérospatiale', *Air & Cosmos*, no. 1220, 14 January 1989, p. 7.

34 Christian Bourdeille, *L'organisation des ventes à l'exportation des grands industriels de l'armement: français, américains, brésiliens et chinois depuis 1945: étude sur les procédures internationales des armements*, PhD dissertation, IEP de Paris, 1990, p. 311.

35 Ulrich Krotz, *Flying Tiger: International Relations Theory and the Politics of Advanced Weapons* (Oxford: Oxford University Press, 2011), p. 135.

36 Martin Lundmark, 'To be or not to be – the integration and the non-integration of the French defence industry', *The FIND Programme*, FOI (Swedish Defence Research Agency), 2004, p. 76, https://www.foi.se/rest-api/report/FOI-R--1291--SE.

37 Vincent Nouzille, 'Contrats: Comment faire sans pots-de-vin …', *L'Express*, 25 February 1999, https://www.lexpress.fr/informations/contrats-comment-faire-sans-pots-de-vin_632789.html.

38 *Ibid.*

39 Alexandra Schwartzbrod, 'Les offices d'armement, intermédiaires et tirelires', *Libération*, 16 July 1996, https://www.liberation.fr/france-archive/1996/07/16/les-offices-d-armement-intermediaires-et-tirelires-lies-au-ministere-de-la-defense-ils-sont-le-passa_176953.

40 Alexandra Schwartzbrod, 'Les Français devront revoir leur méthode', *Libération*, 15 February 1999, https://www.liberation.fr/evenement/1999/02/15/les-francais-devront-revoir-leur-methode-une-loi-permettait-de-deduire-les-pots-de-vin-des-impots-ce_264988.

41 Décret n°2000-521 du 15 juin 2000 portant suppression du contrôle économique et financier de l'État sur certains organismes et entreprises du secteur aéronautique et spatial, *Journal Officiel de la République Française*, no. 139, 17 June 2000, p. 9112, https://www.legifrance.gouv.fr/affichTexte.do?cidTexte=LE-

GITEXT000005629517&date-Texte=20170827.

42 Jean-Pierre Neu, 'L'Etat coupe les ponts avec les offices d'armement', *Les Echos*, 20 March 2001, https://www.lesechos.fr/2001/03/letat-coupe-les-ponts-avec-les-offices-darmement-1052782; Alexandra Schwartzbrod, 'Les Français devront revoir leur méthode'.

43 Laurent Giovachini, *L'armement français au XXème siècle. Une politique à l'épreuve de l'histoire* (Paris: Ellipses, Les Cahiers de l'Armement, 2000), p. 118; Samy Cohen, *La défaite des généraux. Le pouvoir politique et l'armée sous la Vè République* (Paris: Fayard, 1994), p. 242.

44 Sophie Lefeez, *Représentations et usages des armements contemporains: Pour une socio-anthropologie de la complexité technique*, PhD dissertation, Université Paris 1 Panthéon-Sorbonne, 2014, p. 277.

45 Bastien Irondelle, '11. "Qui contrôle le nerf de la guerre?" Financement et politique de défense', pp. 491–523, in Philippe Bezes and Alexandre Siné (eds), *Gouverner (par) les finances publiques* (Paris: Presses de Sciences Po, 2011), pp. 503–04.

46 Interview 68.

47 Jacques Isnard, 'Concurrence effrénée, clientèle insolvable. Des à-coups dans le commerce des armes', *Le Monde*, 23 July 1986, https://www.lemonde.fr/archives/article/1986/07/23/concurrence-effrenee-clientele-insolvable-des-a-coups-dans-le-commerce-des-armes_3117364_1819218.html.

48 Jacques Isnard, 'There are no problems, only solutions', *Defense & Armament*, Héraclès International, no. 65, September 1987, p. 90.

49 Christian Bourdeille, *L'organisation des ventes à l'exportation des grands industriels de l'armement: français, américains, brésiliens et chinois depuis 1945: étude sur les procédures internationales des armements*, PhD dissertation, IEP de Paris, 1990, p. 311.

50 Jacques Isnard, 'Un industriel pour l'État, un fonctionnaire chez Dassault. Chassé-croisé entre vendeurs d'armes', *Le Monde*, 17 May 1990, p. 8, https://www.lemonde.fr/archives/article/1990/05/17/un-industriel-pour-l-etat-un-fonctionnaire-chez-dassault-chasse-croise-entre-vendeurs-d-armes_3960984_1819218.html.

51 Décret no 97-35 du 17 janvier 1997 fixant les attributions et l'organisation de la délégation générale pour l'armement, *Journal Officiel de la République Française*, no. 16, 19 January 1997, p. 965, https://www.legifrance.gouv.fr/affichTexte.do;jsessionid=31D20B2741D380C-C34BD70ECCE62CA0F.tplgfr29s_2?-cidTexte=JORFTEXT000000380757&dateTexte=19970119; Arrêté du 17 janvier 1997 portant organisation de la direction de la coopération et des affaires industrielles, *Journal Officiel de la République Française*, no. 16, 19 January 1997, p. 971, https://www.legifrance.gouv.fr/affichTexte.do?cidTexte=JORFTEXT000000199022&categorieLien=id.

52 Giovanni De Briganti, 'Government moves to support weapons export', *Defense News*, 14–20 October 1996, p. 38.

53 Décret n°2000-807 du 25 août 2000 modifiant le décret n° 92–524 du 16 juin 1992 portant création de la délégation aux affaires stratégiques du ministère de la défense, *Journal Officiel de la République Française*, no. 198, 27 August 2000, p. 13218, text no. 14, https://www.legifrance.gouv.fr/affichTexteArticle.do;jsessionid=31D20B2741D380C-C34BD70ECCE62CA0F.tplgfr29s_2?-cidTexte=JORFTEXT000000357776&idArticle=LEGIARTI000006534966&dateTexte=20200128&categorie-

Lien=id#LEGIARTI000006534966.

54 Organisation for Economic Co-ope-ration and Development (OECD), 'France – Convention de l'OCDE sur la lutte contre la corruption', http://www.oecd.org/fr/daf/anti-corruption/france-conventiondelocdesurlalutte-contrelacorruption.htm.

55 Assemblée Nationale, Commission de la défense nationale et des forces armées, Rapport d'information sur le contrôle des exportations d'armement n°2334, présenté par Jean-Claude Sandrier, Christian Martin et Alain Veryet, 25 April 2000, p. 74, http://www.assemblee-nationale.fr/rap-info/i2334.asp.

56 Alexandra Schwartzbrod, 'Les Français devront revoir leur méthode'.

57 Interview 65.

58 Alexandra Schwartzbrod, 'Les Français devront revoir leur méthode'.

59 *Ibid.*

60 Interview 78.

61 Interview 83.

62 Sénat, Commission affaires étrangères, défense et forces armées du Sénat, Défense Exportations françaises d'équipements militaires, Audition de M. Jean-Bernard Ouvrieu, représentant personnel du ministre de la défense, 1 December 1999, https://www.senat.fr/commission/etr/d_etrg991204.html#toc3.

63 Interview 88.

64 Interview 53.

65 Interview 88.

66 Déclaration sur le rapport sur les exportations d'armement de la France en 1999, les conditions dans lesquelles elles sont exécutées et la réforme des procédures de contrôle de ces exportations, discours de M. Alain Richard, Ministre de la Défense, Paris, 25 April 2001, https://www.vie-publique.fr/discours/178150-declaration-de-m-alain-richard-ministre-de-la-defense-sur-le-rapport.

67 Interview 60.

68 Assemblée Nationale, Commission de la défense nationale et des forces armées, Rapport d'information sur le contrôle des exportations d'armement n°2334, présenté par Jean-Claude Sandrier, Christian Martin et Alain Veryet, 25 April 2000, pp. 99–100, http://www.assemblee-nationale.fr/rap-info/i2334.asp.

69 Bjorn Hagelin, Pieter D. Wezemand and Siemon T. Wezeman, 'Trans-fers of major conventional weapons', *SIPRI Yearbook 1999: Armaments, Disarmament and International Security* (Oxford: Oxford University Press, 1999), p. 439, https://www.sipri.org/sites/default/files/SIPRI%20Yearbook%201999.pdf.

70 Déclaration sur la politique étran-gère, notamment l'engagement euro-péen du gouvernement, la démocratie et les droits de l'homme, et les 'défis globaux' de la communauté internatio-nale, Lionel Jospin, Premier ministre, Paris, 29 August 1997, https://www.vie-publique.fr/discours/176101-decla-ration-de-m-lionel-jospin-premier-mi-nistre-sur-la-politique-etra.

71 Ian Davis, *The Regulation of Arms and Dual-Use Exports: Germany, Sweden and the UK* (Stockholm/Oxford: Stockholm International Peace Research Insti-tute (SIPRI) / Oxford University Press, 2002), p. 101.

72 Bjorn Hagelin, Pieter D. Wezemand and Siemon T. Wezeman, 'Transfers of major conventional weapons', pp. 439–40.

73 Ian Davis, *The Regulation of Arms and Dual-Use Exports: Germany, Sweden and the UK*, p. 101.

74 Sibylle Bauer, *The EU Code of Conduct*

on *Arms Exports – much accom-plished, much to be done*, pp. 31–47, in Karin Haglind (ed.), *Arms Trade: Final report from the 2nd ecumenical conference in Gothenburg* (Sundby-berg: Christian Council of Sweden, 2004), p. 34, https://www.yumpu. com/en/document/view/30233970/ arms-trade-the-gothenburg-process.

75 Susanne T. Hansen, 'Taking ambigu-ity seriously: Explaining the indeter-minacy of the European Union con-ventional arms export control regime', *European Journal of International Rela-tions*, vol. 22, no. 1, 2016, pp. 192–216, p. 206, https://journals.sagepub.com/ doi/pdf/10.1177/1354066115584086.

76 Interview 78.

Chapter Four

1   Kim Willsher, '"Karachi affair": six on trial in France over arms-sales scandal', *Guardian*, 7 October 2019, https://www. theguardian.com/world/2019/oct/07/ french-politicians-to-face-trial-in-arms-sales-corruption-case.

2   'Jean-Claude Mallet, un spécialiste reconnu des questions stratégiques', *Le Figaro*, 24 August 2007, https://www. lefigaro.fr/politique/2007/08/24/01002 -20070824ARTFIG90177-jean_claude_ mallet_un_specialiste_reconnu_des_ questions_strategiques.php.

3   Ministère des Armées, rapports au Par-lament sur les exportations d'arme-ment de la France, 2000–07.

4   Véronique Guillermard and Arnaud De la Grange, 'Morin engage la relance des exportations d'arme-ment', *Le Figaro*, 13 December 2007, https://www.lefigaro.fr/econo-mie/2007/12/13/04001-20071213ART-FIG00322-morin-engage-la-relance-des-exportations-darmements.php; Ministère des Armées, 'Les expor-tations d'armement de la France en 2007', Rapport au Parlement, October 2008, p. 14.

5   SIPRI Arms Transfers Database, 'Importer/exporter TIV tables', http:// armstrade.sipri.org/armstrade/page/ values.php.

6   Paul Holtom, Mark Bromley and Pieter D. Wezeman, '7. International arms transfers', *SIPRI Yearbook 2008: Armaments, Disarmament and Interna-tional Security* (Oxford: Oxford Univer-sity Press, 2008), p. 303, https://www. sipri.org/sites/default/files/YB08%20 293%2007.pdf.

7   Interview 81.

8   Jean-Pierre Neu, 'Les industriels fran-çais de la défense veulent un traite-ment à l'américaine', *Les Echos*, 13 October 2004, https://www.lesechos. fr/2004/10/les-industriels-francais-de-la-defense-veulent-un-traitement-a-la-mericaine-650095.

9   Arnaud De la Grange, 'L'industrie de défense appelle à la mobilisation pour les exportations', *Le Figaro*, 11 July 2007.

10 Interview 48.

11 Interview 79.

12 Laurent Zecchini, 'Un plan pour relancer les exportations d'arme-ment', *Le Monde*, 15 December 2007,

https://www.lemonde.fr/economie/article/2007/12/14/un-plan-pour-relancer-les-exportations-d-armement_989875_3234.html.

13 'Armement: la France perd des munitions à l'export', *La Tribune*, 6 July 2006.

14 Interview 55.

15 Interview 57.

16 'Déclaration sur la politique de défense, notamment en matière d'industrie d'armement', discours de Michèle Alliot-Marie, ministre des Armées, Paris, 11 January 2006, https://discours.vie-publique.fr/discours/159996-declaration-de-mme-michele-alliot-marie-ministre-de-la-defense-sur-la.

17 Yves Fromion, 'Les exportations de défense et de sécurité de la France', 23 June 2006, https://www.vie-publique.fr/sites/default/files/rapport/pdf/064000562.pdf.

18 Alain Ruello, 'Jacques-Emmanuel de Lajugie', *Les Echos*, 18 January 2007, https://www.lesechos.fr/2007/01/jacques-emmanuel-de-lajugie-1073325.

19 Interview 60.

20 *Ibid.*

21 Interview 57.

22 Jean Guisnel, *Armes de corruption massive. Secrets et combines des marchands de canons* (Paris: La Découverte, 2011), pp. 277–78.

23 Damon Mayaffre, *Nicolas Sarkozy. Mesure et démesure du discours* (Paris: Presses de Sciences Po, 2012). See also: 'Le discours de Nicolas Sarkozy à l'université de l'UMP à Marseille', *Le Monde*, 3 September 2006, http://www.lemonde.fr/societe/article/2006/09/03/discours-de-m-sarkozy_809069_3224.html.

24 Jacques de Maillard and Yves Surel, 'Introduction. De la rupture à la présidence ordinaire', in Jacques de Maillard and Yves Surel (eds), *Poli-tiques publiques 3. Les politiques publiques sous Sarkozy* (Paris: Presses de Sciences Po, 2012), pp. 19–20.

25 Interview 38.

26 Interview 57.

27 Interview 65.

28 Interview 60.

29 Jean Liou, 'Mistral: une difficulté de plus pour l'industrie française à l'export', AFP, 20 August 2010.

30 'La "War Room", un outil de décision', *La Tribune*, 9 March 2009, p. 3, https://www.latribune.fr/journal/archives/edition-du-0903/evenement/158021/la-war-room-un-outil-de-decision.html.

31 Solène Davesne and Guillaume Lecompte-Boinet, 'Le coût caché des grands contrats', *L'Usine Nouvelle*, no. 3225, 10 February 2011, pp. 28–31, https://www.usinenouvelle.com/article/le-cout-cache-des-grands-contrats.N146361.

32 Interview 35.

33 Délégation à l'information et à la communication de Défense, 'La stratégie de relance des exportations du ministère de la défense', Ministère des Armées, 13 December 2007, p. 5.

34 Sénat, Projet de loi de finances pour 2013. Défense: environnement et prospective de la politique de défense, Avis n°150 (2012–2013), MM. Jeanny Lorgeoux and André Trillard, 22 November 2012, https://www.senat.fr/rap/a12-150-5/a12-150-5.html.

35 Jean-Michel Gras, 'Témoignage d'un attaché de défense: principes et réalités saoudiennes', *Revue Défense Nationale*, vol. 754, 2012, p. 53, https://www.defnat.com/e-RDN/vue-article.php?carticle=15134.

36 Assemblée Nationale, Rapport d'information n°2469, déposé par la Commission de la Défense Nation-

ale et des Forces Armées, en conclusion des travaux d'une mission d'information sur le dispositif de soutien aux exportations d'armement, Mme Nathalie Chabanne et M. Yves Foulon, 17 December 2014, p. 43, http://www.assemblee-nationale.fr/14/pdf/rap-info/i2469.pdf.

37 Ministère des Armées, Délégation à l'information et à la communication de Défense, 'La stratégie de relance des exportations du ministère de la défense', 13 December 2007, p. 6.

38 Assemblée Nationale, Rapport d'information n°2469, déposé par la Commission de la Défense Nationale et des Forces Armées, en conclusion des travaux d'une mission d'information sur le dispositif de soutien aux exportations d'armement, Mme Nathalie Chabanne et M. Yves Foulon, p. 66.

39 Interview 54.

40 Philippe Japiot, 'Les sociétés d'exportation de défense en appui de l'action de l'État', pp. 26–27, *CAIA, Le magazine des ingénieurs de l'armement*, 'Les exportations de défense', vol. 90, October 2009, p. 27.

41 Hervé Gattegno, 'L'Elysée marchand d'armes', *Le Point*, 24 January 2008, p. 40.

42 Antoine Izambard and Vincent Lamigeon, 'Armement: Parly se plie à la volonté du prince héritier d'Arabie saoudite Mohammed ben Salmane', *Challenges*, 5 April 2018, https://www.challenges.fr/entreprise/defense/armement-parly-se-plie-a-la-volonte-du-prince-heritier-d-arabie-saoudite-mohammed-ben-salmane_578186.

43 Ministère des Armées, 'Les exportations d'armement de la France en 2007', Rapport au Parlement, October 2008, p. 48.

44 Yves Fromion, 'Les exportations de défense et de sécurité de la France',

23 June 2006, https://www.vie-publique.fr/sites/default/files/rapport/pdf/064000562.pdf.

45 Hervé Morin, 'Préface d'Hervé Morin, Ministre de la Défense', *CAIA, Le magazine des ingénieurs de l'armement, 'Les exportations de défense'*, vol. 90, October 2009, pp. 4–5.

46 Ministère de l'Economie et des Finances, Projet de Loi de Finances 2008, Budgets Annexes, Présentation du programme et des actions.

47 Ministère de l'Economie et des Finances, Projet de Loi de Finances 2009 Budgets Annexes, Présentation du programme et des actions.

48 Hervé Morin, 'Préface d'Hervé Morin, Ministre de la Défense', p. 5.

49 Véronique Guillermard and Arnaud De la Grange, 'Morin engage la relance des exportations d'armement'.

50 Assemblée Nationale, Rapport sur les conditions de libération des infirmières et du médecin bulgares détenus en Libye et sur les récents accords franco-libyens, no. 662, 22 January 2008. See Audition conjointe de M. Jean de Ponton d'Amécourt, ancien directeur chargé de la délégation aux affaires stratégiques (DAS) au ministère de la défense, et de l'ingénieur général Jean Hamiot, ancien adjoint au directeur de la délégation aux affaires stratégiques chargé du contrôle des biens et technologies sensibles, de la réflexion en matière de stabilité stratégique et menaces nouvelles, 6 December 2007, http://www.assemblee-nationale.fr/13/pdf/rap-enq/r0622.pdf.

51 Assemblée Nationale, Audition de M. Michel Miraillet, directeur des affaires stratégiques, sur le projet de loi de finances pour 2008, Assemblée Nationale, Commission de la défense nationale et des forces armées, Compte rendu no. 4, Présidence de M. Guy

Teissier, président, 10 October 2007, http://www.assemblee-nationale.fr/13/cr-cdef/07-08/c0708004.asp.

52 'Easing Arms Export Controls?', *Intelligence Online*, 13 December 2007, https://www.intelligenceonline.com/business-intelligence-and-lobbying/2007/12/13/easing-arms-export-controls,35774738-art.

53 Interview 60.

54 Ministère des Armées, 'Défense et Sécurité Nationale: le Livre Blanc', June 2008, p. 279, https://www.defense.gouv.fr/content/download/206186/2286591/file/Livre-blanc-sur-la-Defense-et-la-Securite-nationale%202013.pdf.

55 'Splitting Duties between DAS and DGA', *Intelligence Online*, 24 July 2008, https://www.intelligenceonline.com/corporate-intelligence/2008/07/24/splitting-duties-between-das-and-dga,45817992-art.

56 Ministère des Armées, Rapport au Parlement sur les exportations d'armement de la France en 2006, November 2007, p. 39.

57 Jean-Michel Cédro and Alain Ruello, 'Armement: Michèle Alliot-Marie annonce un plan de soutien à l'export', *Les Echos*, 5 April 2007, p. 20, https://www.lesechos.fr/2007/04/armement-michele-alliot-marie-annonce-un-plan-de-soutien-a-lexport-526730.

58 Ministère des Armées, 'Les exportations d'armement de la France en 2010', Rapport au Parlement, August 2011, p. 50.

59 For a full description of the reform, see Lucie Béraud-Sudreau, 'French adaptation strategies for arms export controls since the 1990s', *Paris Paper*, vol. 10 (Paris: Institut de recherches stratégiques de l'École Militaire, 2014), https://www.defense.gouv.fr/content/download/305828/4086800/file/Paris_paper_n%C2%B010_En.pdf.

60 Sénat, Rapport n°306, Projet de loi relatif au contrôle des importations et des exportations de matériels de guerre et de matériels assimilés, à la simplification des transferts des produits liés à la défense dans l'Union européenne et aux marchés de défense et de sécurité, Josselin De Rohan, 15 February 2011, p. 41, https://www.senat.fr/rap/l10-306/l10-3061.pdf.

61 Interview 55.

62 Interview 86.

63 Interview 61.

64 Yves Fromion, 'Les moyens de développer et de structurer une industrie européenne de défense', 30 June 2008, p. 24, https://www.vie-publique.fr/sites/default/files/rapport/pdf/084000456.pdf.

65 Renaud Dehousse and Anand Menon, 'The French Presidency', *Journal of Common Market Studies*, vol. 47, no. 1, 2009, p. 102.

66 Catherine Hoeffler, *Les politiques d'armement en Europe: l'Adieu aux armes de l'État nation? Une comparaison entre l'Allemagne, la France, le Royaume- Uni et l'Union européenne de 1976 à 2010*, PhD dissertation, IEP de Paris, 2011, pp. 523–24; 'Hervé Morin: Les 27 ne peuvent pas avoir la même ambition', EurActiv.fr, 9 November 2008, http://www.euractiv.fr/institutions/taginstitutions20100208herve-morin-27-ne-peuvent-pas-avoir-meme-ambition_52110-1367.html.

67 Interview 56.

68 Interview 61.

69 Interview 56.

70 Interview 60.

71 Yves Fromion, 'Transposition de la directive européenne simplifiant les transferts intracommunautaires d'équi-

pements de défense. Conséquence du traité de Lisbonne sur les capacités militaires et les programmes d'armement de l'Union Européenne. Conclusions finales de la mission confiée par Monsieur le Premier Ministre', 30 June 2010, http://www.politiquemania.com/pdf/missions-temporaires/rapport-yves-fromion-traite-lisbonne.pdf.

72 Interview 17.

73 Hugo Meijer, 'Transatlantic perspectives on China's military modernization: The case of Europe's arms embargo against the people's Republic of China', *Paris Paper*, vol. 12 (Paris: Institut de recherches stratégiques de l'École Militaire, 2014), p. 23, https://www.defense.gouv.fr/content/download/316927/4301558/file/paris_paper_n_12.pdf.

74 *Ibid.*, p. 23.

75 Interview 61.

76 *Ibid.*

77 *Ibid.*

78 'Arms Transfers to the Middle East and North Africa. Lessons for an Effective Arms Trade Treaty', Amnesty International, 19 October 2011, https://www.amnesty.org/en/documents/act30/117/2011/en/.

79 Nils Duquet, *Business as usual? Assessing the impact of the Arab Spring on European arms export control policies* (Brussels: Flemish Peace Institute, 2014), pp. 15–19, https://vlaamsvredesinstituut.eu/en/report/business-as-usual/.

80 Amnesty International France, CCFD-Terre Solidaire, Oxfam France, 'Projet de loi sur le contrôle du commerce des armes. Les députés vont-ils refuser de tirer les leçons du printemps arabe?', 8 April 2011, https://ccfd-terresolidaire.org/IMG/pdf/cpcontrolearmesloitico8042011.pdf.

81 Assemblée Nationale, 'Séances du mardi 11 janvier 2011, Compte-rendu intégral', *Journal Officiel de la République Française*, p. 8, http://www.assemblee-nationale.fr/13/pdf/cri/2010-2011/20110091.pdf.

82 'Paris blocked riot equipment export as Ben Ali prepared to flee', RFI, 19 January 2011, http://www.rfi.fr/en/africa/20110119-paris-blocked-riot-equipment-export-ben-ali-prepared-flee.

83 Gill Bates and Pieter Wezeman, 'Halte au cynisme! Il faut un commerce des armes plus responsable', *Le Monde*, 21 April 2011, https://www.lemonde.fr/idees/article/2011/04/20/halte-au-cynisme-il-faut-un-commerce-des-armes-plus-responsable_1510356_3232.html.

84 Assemblée Nationale, 'Séances du mardi 12 avril 2011, Compte-rendu intégral', *Journal Officiel de la République Française*, discours de François de Rugy, p. 2458, http://www.assemblee-nationale.fr/13/pdf/cri/2010-2011/20110161.pdf.

85 Sénat, 'Séance du mardi 1er mars 2011, Compte-rendu intégral', *Journal Officiel de la République Française* – see speech by Michelle Demessine, pp. 1653–54, https://www.senat.fr/seances/s201103/s20110301/s20110301.pdf; Assemblée Nationale, 'Séances du mardi 12 avril 2011, Compte-rendu intégral', *Journal Officiel de la République Française* – see speech by Jean-Jacques Candelier, p. 2453, http://www.assemblee-nationale.fr/13/pdf/cri/2010-2011/20110161.pdf; Sénat, 'Séances du mercredi 8 juin 2011, Compte-rendu intégral', *Journal Officiel de la République Française* – see speech by Guy Fischer, p. 4585, https://www.senat.fr/seances/s201106/s20110608/s20110608.pdf.

86 Assemblée Nationale, 'Séances du mardi 12 avril 2011, Compte-rendu

intégral', *Journal Officiel de la République Française* – see speech by Bernard Cazeneuve, pp. 2456–2457, http://www.assemblee-nationale.fr/13/pdf/cri/2010-2011/20110161.pdf.

87 Sénat, Rapport n°536 sur le projet de loi, modifié par l'Assemblée Nationale, relatif au contrôle des importations et des exportations de matériels de guerre et de matériels assimilés, à la simplification des transferts des produits liés à la défense dans l'Union européenne et aux marchés de défense et de sécurité, M. Josselin de Rohan, 18 May 2011, pp. 7–8, https://www.senat.fr/rap/l10-536/l10-5361.pdf.

Chapter Five

1 Michel Cabirol, 'Défense: les cinq paris de la loi de programmation militaire', *La Tribune*, 2 August 2013, https://www.latribune.fr/entreprises-finance/industrie/aeronautique-defense/20130731trib000778429/defense-les-cinq-paris-de-la-loi-de-programmation-militaire.html.

2 Jean Guisnel, 'Loi de programmation militaire: l'export une condition sine qua non!', *Le Point*, 21 January 2015, https://www.lepoint.fr/editos-du-point/jean-guisnel/loi-de-programmation-militaire-l-export-une-condition-sine-qua-non-21-01-2015-1898202_53.php; Vincent Lamigeon, 'Comment Dassault est devenu le meilleur ami de François Hollande', *Challenges*, 5 March 2015, https://www.challenges.fr/entreprise/comment-dassault-est-devenu-le-meilleur-ami-de-francois-hollande_62500.

3 Jean-Dominique Merchet, 'Comment les industriels de la Défense ont fait reculer le gouvernement', *L'Opinion*, 1 June 2014, https://www.lopinion.fr/blog/secret-defense/comment-industriels-defense-ont-fait-reculer-gouvernement-12882.

4 CIDEF, 'L'industrie de défense française 2012', [no date], p. 11, https://www.gifas.asso.fr/fichiersPDF/Actualites/ActualitesGIFAS/Cidef_2012_WEB.pdf.

5 Pierre Tran, 'Priority for French Industry: Exports', *Defense News*, 8 July 2012.

6 Anne Eveno, 'Le VRP Fabius irrite Bercy', *Le Monde*, 9 January 2014, https://www.lemonde.fr/economie/article/2014/01/09/le-vrp-fabius-irrite-bercy_4345081_3234.html.

7 Ministère des Armées, Rapport au Parlement 2014 sur les exportations d'armement de la France, June 2015, p. 12, https://www.defense.gouv.fr/content/download/305478/4080769/file/Rapport%20au%20Parlement%202014%20sur%20les%20exportations%20d/'armement%20de%20la%20France.pdf.

8 Interview 38.

9 'Jean-Yves Le Drian, après sa visite aux Emirats: "Les Rafale (de Dassault) attendront"', *Challenges*, 24 October 2012, https://www.challenges.fr/entreprise/jean-yves-le-drian-apres-sa-visite-aux-emirats-les-rafale-de-dassault-attendront_4744.

10 Jean-Dominique Merchet, 'Jean-Yves Le Drian, le politique du business', *L'Opinion*, 26 July 2013.

11 Assemblée Nationale, Rapport d'information no. 2469, déposé par la Commission de la Défense Nationale et des Forces Armées, en conclusion des travaux d'une mission d'information sur le dispositif de soutien aux exportations d'armement, et présenté par Mme Nathalie Chabanne et M. Yves Foulon, 17 December 2014, p. 41, http://www.assemblee-nationale.fr/14/rapinfo/i2469.asp.

12 Ministère des Armées, Arrêté portant création d'un comité ministériel des exportations de défense, Bulletin officiel des Armées, 2 May 2013, https://www.bo.sga.defense.gouv.fr/texte/78504/Sans%20nom.html.

13 Interview 57.

14 Solène Davesne and Guillaume Lecompte-Boinet, 'Le coût caché des grands contrats', L'Usine Nouvelle, 10 February 2011, https://www.usinenouvelle.com/article/le-cout-cache-des-grands-contrats.N146361.

15 Interview 22.

16 Interview 65.

17 Jean Guisnel, 'Pourquoi les mégacontrats nous échappent', Le Point, 28 January 2010.

18 Interview 57.

19 Interview 65.

20 Jean-Pierer Langellier and Arnaud Leparmentier, 'Le Brésil s'engage à acheter 36 avions français Rafale', Le Monde, 9 September 2009, https://www.lemonde.fr/ameriques/article/2009/09/08/le-bresil-s-engage-a-negocier-l-achat-de-trente-six-avions-rafale_1237432_3222.html; Jean Guisnel and Philippe Mathon, 'Dassault sur son nuage', Le Point, 10 September 2009.

21 'F-X2: Brazil's Saab Contract for Gripen's a Done Deal', Defense Industry Daily, 8 April 2019, http://www.defenseindustrydaily.com/brazil-embarking-upon-f-x2-fighter-program-04179/.

22 Interview 69.

23 Interview 65.

24 Arrêté du 2 janvier 2015 relatif à l'organisation de la direction générale des relations internationales et de la stratégie du ministère de la défense, Journal Officiel de la République Française, 4 January 2015, https://www.legifrance.gouv.fr/affichTexte.do?cidTexte=JORFTEXT000030026996.

25 Jean-Dominique Merchet, 'A la Défense, les relations internationales ont leur direction générale', L'Opinion, 17 December 2014, https://www.lopinion.fr/blog/secret-defense/a-defense-relations-internationales-ont-leur-direction-generale-actualise-19508.

26 Jean Guisnel, 'Le Drian décide de réorganiser son ministère', Le Point, 17 July 2013, https://www.lepoint.fr/editos-du-point/jean-guisnel/le-drian-decide-de-reorganiser-son-ministere-17-07-2013-1705820_53.php.

27 Jean-Dominique Merchet, 'L'état-major des armées perd les ressourcesh umaines et les relations internationales', L'Opinion, 25 June 2013, https://www.lopinion.fr/blog/secret-defense/l-etat-major-armees-perd-ressources-humaines-relations-internationales-1385.

28 Jean Guisnel, 'Document exclusif. L'amiral Guillaud aurait-il dû démissionner', Le Point, 18 July 2013, http://www.lepoint.fr/editos-du-point/jean-guisnel/document-exclusif-l-amiral-guillaud-aurait-du-demissionner-18-07-2013-1706131_53.php. Document attached to the following article: Ministère des Armées, 'Relevé de décisions des comités exécutifs des 30 mai 2013 et 12 juin 2013 sous la présidence

du ministre de la défense', 1 July 2013, no. 6991/DEF/CAD, p. 9.

29 Déclaration sur les exportations de Défense, discours de Jean-Yves Le Drian, ministre des Armées, Bordeaux, 9 September 2014, https://vie-publique. fr/discours/192410-declaration-de-m-jean-yves-le-drian-ministre-de-la-de-fense-sur-les-ex.

30 Arrêté du 2 décembre 2009 relatif à l'organisation de la direction générale de l'armement, Titre IV: Direction du développement international, Cha-pitre 1er: Les sous-directions à com-pétence géographique, Article 35, modifié par arrêté du 7 janvier 2015 - art. 15.

31 Arrêté du 2 décembre 2009 relatif à l'organisation de la direction générale de l'armement, Version consolidée au 29 septembre 2015, Titre III: Direction de la stratégie, Chapitre III: la sous-direction de la coopération et du dével-oppement européen (abrogated).

32 Institut des Hautes Études de Défense Nationale (IHEDN), 'Sociétés de projet, externalisation et ESSD: la défense contrainte de recourir au secteur privé? Entretien avec Guillaume Farde', January 2015, http://www.anaj-ihedn. org/societes-de-projet-externalisation-et-essd-la-defense-contrainte-de-re-courir-au-secteur-prive/.

33 Philippe Chapleau, 'Défense Conseil International réorganise ses antennes régionales', *Lignes de Défense*, 9 Decem-ber 2014, http://lignesdedefense.blogs. ouest-france.fr/archive/2014/12/08/ dci-reorganise-ses-antennes-region-ales-13073.html.

34 François Hollande, 'Perspectives de défense nationale', *Revue Défense Nationale*, no. 749, April 2012, pp. 25–26, https://www.defnat.com/e-RDN/ vue-article.php?carticle=9797.

35 See 'Speech to the General Assembly of the United Nations', François Hollande, President of the Republic, New York, 25 September 2012, https://onu.deleg-france.org/25-septembre-2012-Debat-d.

36 Ministère des Armées, Rapport au Par-lement 2012 sur les exportations d'ar-mement de la France, October 2012, p. 5.

37 Amnesty International, 'Embargo sur les armes: un projet de loi en demi-teinte', 20 January 2015, http://noelma-mere.eelv.fr/embargo-sur-les-armes-un-projet-de-loi-en-demi-teinte/.

38 Tony Fortin, 'Embargo sur les armes: comment la France organise son impu-nité', L'Observatoire des armements, 9 October 2015, http://obsarm.org/spip. php?article256; 'La France avance sur la pénalisation de violations d'embar-gos', *France Soir*, 28 January 2016, http:// www.francesoir.fr/politique-france/ la-france-avance-sur-la-penalisa-tion-de-violations-dembargos.

39 Sénat, Projet de loi relatif à la violation des embargos et autres mesures res-trictives. Les étapes de la discussion, https://www.senat.fr/dossier-legislatif/ pjl05-205.html.

40 Ministère des Armées, 'Contrôle des biens et technologies à double-usage', 24 June 2016, http://www.defense. gouv.fr/dgris/enjeux-transverses/ lutte-contre-la-proliferation/controle-des-biens-et-technologies-a-double-usage.

41 François Hollande, 'Perspectives de défense nationale', *Revue Défense Natio-nale*, no. 749, April 2012, p. 26.

42 Livre blanc sur la Défense et la Sécu-rité Nationale, 2013, p. 127, https:// www.defense.gouv.fr/english/por-tail-defense/issues2/defence-po-licy/le-livre-blanc-sur-la-defense-et-la-securite-nationale-2013/ livre-blanc-2013.

43 Premier Ministre Jean-Marc Ayrault, Lettre de Mission à Monsieur Alain Hespel, Président de la Cour des Comptes, 21 June 2013.

44 Master 2 Droit des Activités Spatiales et des Télécommunications, les 'Dastuces' de la semaine, 8–14 April 2014, http://www.idest-paris.org/revuedepresse/IDEST_Revue_de_Presse_25.pdf.

45 Interview 73.

46 Ibid.

47 Interview 28.

48 Interview 25.

49 Interview 39.

50 Interview 73.

51 'La Russie s'intéresse au BPC Mistral', TTU Lettre d'informations stratégiques et de défense, 5 November 2008, http://web.archive.org/web/20081113083110/http://www.ttu.fr/francais/Articles/bpc-mistralrussie.html.

52 'French May Sell Mistral Class Ships to Russia', 17 November 2009, released by WikiLeaks as Cable 09PARIS1529_a, https://wikileaks.org/plusd/cables/09PARIS1529_a.html.

53 Isabelle Lasserre, 'France-Russie: le nouvel axe strategique', Le Figaro, 24 May 2011, http://www.lefigaro.fr/monfigaro/2011/05/24/10001-20110524ARTFIG00661-france-russie-le-nouvel-axe-strategique.php.

54 'Morin défend à l'Onu le projet de vente de "Mistral" à Moscou', L'Express, 17 September 2010, https://lexpansion.lexpress.fr/actualite-economique/morin-defend-a-l-onu-le-projet-de-vente-de-mistral-a-moscou_1420237.html.

55 Emmanuel Guimard, 'Le président de la République s'engage sur la pérennité du chantier de Saint-Nazaire', Les Echos, 8 September 2008, https://www.lesechos.fr/08/09/2008/LesEchos/20252-080-ECH_le-president-de-la-republique-s-engage-sur-la-perennite-du-chantier-de-saint-nazaire.htm.

56 Philippe Schwab, 'Mistral, éolien: le ciel s'éclaircit pour STX mais la prudence reste de mise', AFP, 25 January 2011.

57 'La vente d'un navire français Mistral à Moscou inquiète au Congrès américain', AFP, 18 December 2009; 'Sarkozy's political gift to Medvedev', Intelligence Online, no. 609, 14 January 2010, https://www.intelligenceonline.com/government-intelligence/2010/01/14/sarkozy-s-political-gift-to-medvedev,78225319-eve.

58 'Entretien Sarkozy-Gates sur fond de ventes de Mistral à la Russie', Associated Press, 8 February 2010.

59 'WikiLeaks: "inquiétudes" américaines sur la vente de Mistral à la Russie', AFP, 29 November 2010.

60 'French May Sell Mistral Class Ships to Russia', 11 November 2009, released by WikiLeaks as Cable 09PARIS1529_a, https://wikileaks.org/plusd/cables/09PARIS1529_a.html.

61 'Georgia: Mistral sale could Destabilize Black Sea', 19 November 2009, released by WikiLeaks as Cable 09TBILISI2025_a, https://wikileaks.org/plusd/cables/09TBILISI2025_a.html; 'Lobbyists try to torpedo Mistral', Intelligence Online, no. 613, 11 March 2010, https://www.intelligenceonline.com/corporate-intelligence/2010/03/11/lobbyists-try-to-torpedo-mistral,82105109-art.

62 Isabelle Lasserre, 'Vente de Mistral à la Russie: les dessous d'un marchandage', Le Figaro, 7 September 2010, http://www.lefigaro.fr/international/2010/09/07/01003-20100907ARTFIG00692-vente-de-mistral-a-la-russie-les-dessous-d-un-marchandage.php.

63 'French May Sell Mistral Class Ships to Russia', 11 November 2009, released by WikiLeaks as Cable

09PARIS1529_a, https://wikileaks.org/plusd/cables/09PARIS1529_a.html.

64 See 'Interview on the situation in Ukraine', interview with Laurent Fabius, Minister of Foreign Affairs, Paris, TF1, 17 March 2014, https://www.vie-publique.fr/discours/190721-entretien-de-m-laurent-fabius-ministre-des-affaires-etrangeres-avec-t.

65 Council of the European Union, 'EU restrictive measures in view of the situation in Eastern Ukraine and the illegal annexation of Crimea', 29 July 2014, https://www.consilium.europa.eu/media/22023/144159.pdf.

66 Jean Guisnel, 'Mistral à la Russie: Après avoir énervé nos alliés, on va énerver les Russes', Le Point, 4 September 2014, http://www.lepoint.fr/editos-du-point/jean-guisnel/la-france-ne-livrera-pas-de-mistral-a-la-russie-03-09-2014-1859814_53.php.

67 Yves-Michel Riols, Nathalie Guibert and Isabelle Mandraud, 'La Russie accentue la pression sur la France pour obtenir la livraison des Mistral', Le Monde, 14 November 2014, https://www.lemonde.fr/europe/article/2014/11/14/la-russie-accentue-la-pression-sur-la-france-pour-obtenir-la-livraison-des-mistral_4523633_3214.html.

68 Elizabeth Pineau, 'La France reporte sine die la livraison du Mistral à la Russie', Reuters, 25 November 2014, https://fr.reuters.com/article/newsOne/idFRKCN0J914220141125.

69 Pierre Tran, 'French Mistral Sale Strategy: Buy Time to Maneuver', Defense News, 6 September 2014; Jean-Dominique Merchet, 'Ventes d'armes: sous l'affaire du Mistral, l'exportation du Rafale', L'Opinion, 3 September 2014, https://www.lopinion.fr/blog/secret-defense/ventes-d-armes-l-affaire-mistral-l-exportation-

rafale-15937; Laurent Lagneau, 'Le feuilleton des Mistral russes n'aura pas de conséquence sur la vente de 126 Rafale à l'Inde', Opex 360.com, 28 November 2014, http://www.opex360.com/2014/11/28/le-feuilleton-des-mistral-russes-naura-pas-de-consequence-sur-la-vente-de-126-rafale-linde/.

70 Damien Brunon, 'Nouveau contrat pour les chantiers navals STX de St Nazaire, Europe-1, 9 May 2014, https://www.europe1.fr/economie/Nouveau-contrat-pour-les-chantiers-navals-STX-de-St-Nazaire-853804.

71 Assemblée Nationale, Commission des Affaires étrangères, Audition de M. Laurent Fabius, ministre des affaires étrangères et du développement international, sur le projet de loi sur la cessation de l'accord de coopération avec la Russie dans le domaine de la construction de bâtiments de projection et de commandement, compte-rendu, 15 September 2015, http://www.assemblee-nationale.fr/14/cr-cafe/14-15/c1415100.asp.

72 Vincent Jauvert, 'Mistral: comment Sarkozy et Fillon ont cédé aux exigences russes', L'Obs, 10 August 2014, https://www.nouvelobs.com/l-enquete-de-l-obs/20140806.OBS5698/mistral-comment-sarkozy-et-fillon-ont-cede-aux-exigences-russes.html.

73 'Ukraine Expects France to Wriggle Out of Russia Warship Delivery', Defense News, 17 November 2014.

74 'Poland Says French–Russian Warship Deal Raises Issues for Missile Shield', Defense News, 29 September 2014.

75 Nathalie Guibert, Dominique Gallois and Marie-Béatrice Baudet, 'Rafale, les coulisses de l'exploit', Le Monde, 29 May 2015, https://www.lemonde.fr/idees/article/2015/05/29/rafale-les-coulisses-de-l-exploit_4643804_3232.html.

76 Christophe Ayad, 'François (Hollande) d'Arabie', *Le Monde*, 30 April 2015, https://www.lemonde.fr/idees/article/2015/04/30/francois-d-arabie_4625576_3232.html; 'Contracts for Fabius, Le Drian, Macron', *Intelligence Online*, 8 April 2015, https://www.intelligenceonline.com/government-intelligence/2015/04/08/contracts-for-fabius-le-drian-macron,108068725-art; Michel Sailhan, 'French courtship of Gulf monarchies is risky: experts', Yahoo News/AFP, 6 May 2015, https://www.yahoo.com/news/french-courtship-gulf-monarchies-risky-experts-152941074.html?ref=gs.

77 Jean-Dominique Merchet, 'Yémen: la tentation française d'intervenir en soutien de l'Arabie Saoudite', *L'Opinion*, 15–16 April 2015, https://www.lopinion.fr/edition/international/yemen-tentation-francaise-d-intervenir-en-soutien-l-arabie-saoudite-23330.

78 Ministère des Armées, Rapport au Parlement 2014 sur les exportations d'armement de la France, August 2014, p. 14.

79 Michel Cabirol, 'Thales remporte un nouveau contrat de support de missiles Crotale en Arabie saoudite', *La Tribune*, 26 March 2013, https://www.latribune.fr/entreprises-finance/industrie/aeronautique-defense/20130325trib000755893/thales-remporte-un-nouveau-contrat-de-support-de-missiles-crotale-en-arabie-saoudite.html.

80 Michel Cabirol, 'La France signe un contrat de plus d'un milliard d'euros avec l'Arabie Saoudite', *La Tribune*, 28 August 2013, https://www.latribune.fr/entreprises-finance/industrie/aeronautique-defense/20130828trib000782031/la-france-signe-un-contrat-de-plus-d-un-milliard-d-euros-avec-l-arabie-saoudite.html.

81 Michel Cabirol, 'Pourquoi Thales est tout près de signer un mégacontrat de 2.5 milliards d'euros en Arabie Saoudite', *La Tribune*, 5 October 2013, https://www.latribune.fr/entreprises-finance/industrie/aeronautique-defense/20131005trib000788372/pourquoi-thales-est-tout-pres-de-signer-un-megacontrat-de-25-milliards-d-euros-en-arabie-saoudite.html.

82 'Lebanon: Paris plays down Saudi gift', *Intelligence Online*, 22 January 2014, https://www.intelligenceonline.com/grey-areas/2014/01/22/lebanon-paris-plays-down-saudi-gift,108004473-art.

83 Awad Mustafa, 'Saudi Arabia cancels $3bn aid to Lebanon; French weapons deal held', *Defense News*, 19 February 2016, https://www.defensenews.com/breaking-news/2016/02/19/saudi-arabia-cancels-3b-aid-to-lebanon-french-weapons-deal-held/.

84 'Mistral Joins Egyptian Buys of French Gear', *Defense News*, 27 September 2015, http://www.defensenews.com/story/defense/naval/ships/2015/09/27/mistral-joins-egyptian-buys-french-gear/72821000/; Hélène Sallon, 'Mistral: l'Arabie Saoudite et l'Egypte "sont prêtes à tout pour acheter les deux navires"', *Le Monde*, 7 August 2015, http://www.lemonde.fr/afrique/article/2015/08/07/l-egypte-et-l-arabie-saoudite-candidates-au-rachat-des-mistrals_4715520_3212.html.

85 'Franco-Belgian CaMo project: Entry into Force of the Intergovernmental Agreement and Contract for the Acquisition of Armored Vehicles', defense-aerospace.com, 28 June 2019, http://www.defense-aerospace.com/articles-view/release/3/203990/belgium's-scorpion-contract-for-french-afvs-comes-into-force.html.

86 Anne Bauer, 'Naval: les Emirats achètent

deux corvettes à la France', *Les Echos*, 9 November 2017, https://www.lesechos.fr/2017/11/naval-les-emirats-achetent-deux-corvettes-a-la-france-187561.

[87] Jean Guisnel, 'Ventes d'armes. Le jeu trouble de la France', *Le Télégramme*, 6 April 2018, https://www.letelegramme.fr/monde/ventes-d-armes-un-cas-de-conscience-06-04-2018-11915545.php.

Conclusion

[1] 'Transformation de la DGA', discours de Florence Parly, ministre des Armées, 5 July 2018, https://www.defense.gouv.fr/salle-de-presse/discours/discours-de-florence-parly/discours_balard_05-07-2018_transformation_dga.

[2] Edward A. Kolodziej, *Making and Marketing Arms: The French Experience and Its Implications for the International System* (Princeton, NJ: Princeton University Press, 1987), p. 83.

[3] Anne Poiret, 'Mon pays fabrique des armes', *Le monde en face*, France 5, 23 October 2019, https://www.francetelevisions.fr/mon-pays-fabrique-des-armes; http://talwegproduction.com/films/mon-pays-fabrique-des-armes/.

[4] Commons Select Committee, 'Chairs urge UK government to reconsider selling arms to Saudi Arabia', 15 December 2016, https://www.parliament.uk/business/committees/committees-a-z/commons-select/international-development-committee/news-parliament-20151/uk-arms-sales-to-saudi-arabia-publication-16-17/.

[5] Court of Appeal, 'The Queen (on the application of Campaign Against Arms Trade) -v- Secretary of State for International Trade and others', 20 June 2019, https://www.judiciary.uk/judgments/the-queen-on-the-applica-tion-of-campaign-against-arms-trade-v-secretary-of-state-for-international-trade-and-others/.

[6] Department for International Trade, 'Notice to exporters 2019/09: Court of Appeal judgment about military exports to Saudi Arabia', 25 June 2019, https://www.gov.uk/government/publications/notice-to-export-ers-201909-court-of-appeal-judgment-about-military-exports-to-saudi-ara-bia/notice-to-exporters-201909-court-of-appeal-judgment-about-military-exports-to-saudi-arabia.

[7] Letter from the Secretary of State for International Trade & President of the Board of Trade to the Chair of the Committees on Arms Export Controls, 16 September 2019, https://assets.publishing.service.gov.uk/government/uploads/system/uploads/attachment_data/file/831880/CAEC_Letter_16092019_1550_Format-ted_-_GS.pdf.

[8] 'Prodotto in Europa, bombardato in Yemen', Rete Italiana per il Disarmo, 12 December 2019, https://www.disarmo.org/rete/a/47120.html.

[9] Amnesty France, 'Armes au Yémen: La France mise en cause', 20 March 2018, https://www.amnesty.fr/controle-des-armes/actualites/armes-au-yemen-la-france-mise-en-cause.

10   Assemblée Nationale, Contrôle des exportations d'armement, http://www2.assemblee-nationale. fr/15/commissions-permanentes/ commission-des-affaires-etran-geres/missions-d-information/ controle-des-exportations-d-armement/ (block)/55065.

11   Disclose, 'Yemeni Papers', 16 April 2019, https://made-in-france.disclose. ngo/en/chapter/yemen-papers.

12   European Parliament, Position of the European Parliament adopted at first reading on 18 April 2019 with a view to the adoption of Regulation (EU) of the European Parliament and of the Council establishing the European Defence Fund, Article 22, paragraph 8a, 18 April 2019, http://www. europarl.europa.eu/doceo/document/ TA-8-2019-0430_EN.html#title2.

13   Lucie Béraud-Sudreau, 'War in Yemen: European divisions on arms-export controls', *Military Balance* Blog, 20 March 2018, https://www.iiss.org/ blogs/military-balance/2018/03/war-yemen-european-arms-export; 'War in Yemen: European divisions on arms-export controls continue', *Military Balance* Blog, 25 October 2018, https:// www.iiss.org/blogs/military-bal-ance/2018/10/yemen-arms-export-divi-sions-continue.

14   Sozialdemokratische Partei Deutschlands (SPD), 'Hamburg Programme 2007. Principal Guidelines of the Social Democratic Party of Germany', 28 October 2007, p. 14, https://www.spd. de/fileadmin/Dokumente/Beschluesse/ Grundsatzprogramme/hamburger_ programm_englisch.pdf; Miljöpartiet de gröna, Party Programme in English, [no date], p. 35, https://www.mp.se/ sites/default/files/mp_partiprogram_ english.pdf.

15   Laurent Lagneau, 'Berlin met des bâtons dans les roues de Nexter', opex360.com, 22 December 2012, http://www.opex360.com/2012/12/22/ berlin-met-des-batons-dans-les-roues-de-nexter/.

16   'Un premier pas', *TTU Lettre d'informations stratégiques et de défense*, 26 January 2015, https://www.ttu.fr/expor-tations-franco-allemandes-un-pre-mier-pas/; Jean-Dominique Merchet, 'L'industrie française de l'armement est l'otage de la coalition allemande', *L'Opinion*, 27 October 2014, https://www. lopinion.fr/blog/secret-defense/l-indus-trie-francaise-l-armement-est-l-otage-coalition-allemande-17749.

17   Michel Cabirol, 'Eurofighter, A330 MRTT, Casa C295, H145 ... bloqués à l'export: Berlin fragilise Airbus', *La Tribune*, 25 February 2019, https:// www.latribune.fr/entreprises-finance/ industrie/aeronautique-defense/euro-fighter-a330-mrtt-casa-c295-h145-bloques-a-l-export-berlin-fragilise-air-bus-808239.html.

18   Florence Parly, ministre des Armées, Compte rendu no. 27, Commission de la defense et des forces armées, Assemblée Nationale, 8 February 2018, http://www.assemblee-nationale.fr/15/ cr-cdef/17-18/c1718027.asp.

19   'Accord entre le Gouvernement de la république fédérale d'Allemagne et le Gouvernement de la république française sur les exportations vers les pays tiers des matériels d'armement développés et/ou produits en coopération'. The full text of the agreement is available (in French) as an appendix to Jean-Claude Sandrier, Christian Martin and Alain Veyret, 'Contrôle des exportations d'armement', Rapport d'information déposé par la Commission de la Défense Nation-

ale et des Forces Armées, Assemblée Nationale, 25 April 2000, http://www.assemblee-nationale.fr/rap-info/i2334.asp.

[20] Ministère de l'Europe et des Affaires Etrangères, 'Accord franco-allemand relatif au contrôle des exportations en matière de défense', 23 October 2019, https://www.diplomatie.gouv.fr/fr/dossiers-pays/allemagne/evenements/article/allemagne-accord-franco-allemand-relatif-au-controle-des-exportations-en; Access to the document: https://www.diplomatie.gouv.fr/IMG/pdf/accord_cle42111e.pdf.

[21] 'Which countries export arms to Turkey?', BBC, 23 October 2019, https://www.bbc.co.uk/news/50125405.

INDEX

Adelphi books are published six times a year by Routledge Journals, an imprint of Taylor & Francis, 4 Park Square, Milton Park, Abingdon, Oxfordshire OX14 4RN, UK.

A subscription to the institution print edition, ISSN 1944-5571, includes free access for any number of concurrent users across a local area network to the online edition, ISSN 1944-558X. Taylor & Francis has a flexible approach to subscriptions enabling us to match individual libraries' requirements. This journal is available via a traditional institutional subscription (either print with free online access, or online-only at a discount) or as part of our libraries, subject collections or archives. For more information on our sales packages please visit www.tandfonline.com/page/librarians.

2020 Annual Adelphi Subscription Rates			
Institution	£832	US$1,459	€1,230
Individual	£285	US$488	€390
Online only	£707	US$1,240	€1,045

Dollar rates apply to subscribers outside Europe. Euro rates apply to all subscribers in Europe except the UK and the Republic of Ireland where the pound sterling price applies. All subscriptions are payable in advance and all rates include postage. Journals are sent by air to the USA, Canada, Mexico, India, Japan and Australasia. Subscriptions are entered on an annual basis, i.e. January to December. Payment may be made by sterling cheque, dollar cheque, international money order, National Giro, or credit card (Amex, Visa, Mastercard).

For a complete and up-to-date guide to Taylor & Francis journals and books publishing programmes, and details of advertising in our journals, visit our website: **http://www.tandfonline.com.**

Ordering information:
USA/Canada: Taylor & Francis Inc., Journals Department, 530 Walnut Street, Suite 850, Philadelphia, PA 19106, USA. **UK/Europe/Rest of World:** Routledge Journals, T&F Customer Services, T&F Informa UK Ltd., Sheepen Place, Colchester, Essex, CO3 3LP, UK.

Advertising enquiries to:
USA/Canada: The Advertising Manager, Taylor & Francis Inc., 530 Walnut Street, Suite 850, Philadelphia, PA 19106, USA. Tel: +1 (800) 354 1420. Fax: +1 (215) 207 0050. **UK/Europe/Rest of World**: The Advertising Manager, Routledge Journals, Taylor & Francis, 4 Park Square, Milton Park, Abingdon, Oxfordshire OX14 4RN, UK. Tel: +44 (0) 20 7017 6000. Fax: +44 (0) 20 7017 6336.